LEADING TEAMS

How to Inspire, Motivate, Lead and Succeed!

LEADING TEAMS

How to Inspire, Motivate, Lead and Succeed!

James Dyke

SkillPath® Publications

Editor: Bill Cowles

Layout and cover design: Jason Sprenger

ISBN: 978-1-934589-00-7

10 9 8 7 6 5 4 3 2   07   08   09   10

Printed in the United States of America

TABLE OF CONTENTS

PART I:
Inspire—Channeling Your Leadership Power

PART II:
Motivate—Igniting Your Team's Personal Passion

PART III:
Lead—Achieving World-class Performance

PART IV:
Succeed—Receiving Recognition, Reward, Raises and Rank

INTRODUCTION

Congratulations on acquiring this valuable resource! You hold in your hands a personal guide to your leadership success—a balanced offering of keen insight and practical tools that will enable you to lead others well and experience personal success in the process.

PART I: Inspire—will equip you to become a leader who uses influence to inspire others to maximum performance. Each of its seven chapters supplies an important piece of the puzzle that ultimately provides you with a strategy for becoming an inspiration to your team members—able to exert powerful and charismatic influence as a leader.

PART II: Motivate—tackles the tough challenge of worker motivation and shows you how to tap into the personal passions of your team members and channel those passions into high performance and enthusiastic engagement. You'll also discover practical ways you can feed that fire of inspiration with recognition and reward—and create a dynamic team culture that attracts and keeps the very best workers.

PART III: Lead—gives you practical strategies for building a creative and collaborative team that delivers high productivity and "Superstar" performance. You'll learn the essentials to achieving team success and how using those essentials will enable you to solve problems, overcome difficult circumstances and transform counterproductive behavior.

PART IV: Succeed—completes the picture by coaching you to personal and professional success. Use the valuable tips to identify your real job and learn how to garner the support of higher-ups to open doors of opportunity for personal advancement and promotion. Learn how to turbocharge your career and accomplish your most cherished professional goals.

Don't just read this book—use it! Each section is supported by real-life stories and valuable action steps that will give you tangible and practical ways to immediately apply the principles and tips. Plan now on setting aside time to use these practical suggestions to move your career forward and put yourself on the pathway to achievement and success. Don't wait another moment to start making a difference in your leadership and your career.

PART I:

Inspire—Channeling Your Leadership Power

The secret of inspiration is really quite simple: Great leaders have always inspired people with the example of their own life—their behavior, their activities and their choices. This is a universal principle of learning and life. It's called "modeling," and some researchers claim that it's the *only* way we learn anything in life!

You can put this claim to the test right now. Think of a good manager, boss or supervisor you have worked for at some point in your life. What did this person do that enabled you to be effective in your work and even enjoy your working relationship? (If you like, take out a separate piece of paper and write down your insights.) There is a good chance that your list will include (a) behaviors that you are trying to use in your own work as a supervisor and (b) behaviors that researchers have associated with effective leadership. This is a perfect example of how the behavior of an effective leader impacts others: It influences people to follow the leader's example, and it teaches people how to become good leaders themselves. This is why it's often said that great leaders don't create followers—they create other leaders.

How do you inspire people to follow you? How do you influence others through your model of leadership? It's simple when you follow the simple path to greater leadership by channeling the power of your personal influence and using the building blocks outlined in this helpful and practical section.

CHAPTER 1:

Acquiring respect

It should be obvious to any manager or supervisor acquainted with contemporary culture: You can no longer assume that you'll automatically be respected by your team! You'll have to *earn* the respect of your people—through meticulous behavior and a respectful mindset of your own. Follow these simple suggestions and you'll establish yourself as a leader who is worthy of respect.

Treat others with respect

Yes, respectful behavior begins with *you*. It means addressing people with respect whenever you communicate with them; using simple courtesies in daily communication; giving others your full attention when talking and listening; using "please," "thank you" and "excuse me" appropriately; and displaying high regard in every personal interaction—whether giving assignments, explaining instructions, offering correction or enforcing discipline. It also means demonstrating the same respectful behavior to anyone in any situation, regardless of rank, authority, position or influence. How important is this? Very important, according to a recent study in the workplace that revealed 80% of workers today say that they "get no respect at work." And the indicators of respect are behavioral—another study listed the top "pet peeves" of workers today: 44% complained of "being spoken to in a condescending tone"; 37% identified "experiencing a public reprimand"; and 34% complained of "being micromanaged." You can address the need for respect in the workplace and become a leader who commands respect simply by demonstrating respect for others in the way you treat them.

Act with integrity

In the current era of business, values and ethics have taken on fresh significance. The behavior of leaders is paramount in this regard—workers will not respect leaders who break the rules or break the law. And workers will have little patience with leaders who apply high standards of performance and excellence for their teams but are unwilling to apply the same standards to themselves. Workers everywhere have a keen desire for fairness in the workplace. That calls for managers to apply rules and standards consistently without favoritism. And that also means not bending the rules for other leaders, managers and supervisors. Yes, workers understand that "rank has its privileges"—that managers and higher-ups are entitled to certain advantages and "perks." But workers will not tolerate anything that has the appearance of laxity or duplicity—they expect their boss to conform to the same corporate standards, rules and guidelines that they do, with no exceptions for position, power or hierarchy. Leader be warned: Any attempt on your part to shortchange the organization, the client, the workers or the shareholders; any breach of trust or ethics; any hint of partiality or bias; any abuse of power or position (especially for personal gain) will destroy the respect of your team and irreparably damage your influence and authority.

Listen

Yes, listen! It's one of the most powerful ways you communicate value and respect to your people. To begin with, it sends the message to your people that they matter … they count … they are important. Think of how you feel when someone with position, prestige or authority genuinely seeks your opinion. Think of how you feel when someone important asks you the simple question, "What do you think?" Your people feel the same way whenever you ask them the same question.

So, ask and learn! Use the answers you receive from your team members to help you make better assessments, craft better decisions, design better solutions and create better leadership. Why? Because listening is one of the most important avenues to learning. When you begin to ask and listen, you open the doors to wisdom and productivity. Asking for your team's input enfranchises their creativity and innovation (more about that later). It releases the flow of good ideas. It creates ownership and buy-in. And … it attracts people to your leadership! If you have any doubt, think of the opposite approach—this autocratic response to a worker's ideas: *You're not getting paid to think. You're getting paid to work. So shut up and get back to work.* This opposite, autocratic approach communicates disrespect and leads to worker disengagement, lower productivity and loss of ownership and accountability. Listening is a powerful antidote to abusive, autocratic management—it builds respect, engages ownership and energizes worker initiative.

Effective and respectful listening also sets the tone for your team's behavior. It shows them how to do the same—how to listen carefully, openly, genuinely and respectfully. Once again, your behavior becomes a model to help you teach and train your team and show them how to develop the same important skill. This will not just teach them how to listen to you more receptively (although that in itself is a valuable result)—it will also teach them how to listen to one another more effectively—and that creates better team communication and greater team cohesion.

Finally, when you take time to listen to your people, you score big with them in the "fairness" column. It's a simple case of reciprocity—if *you* want *them* to listen to *you*, *you* have to be willing to listen to *them*. Fair is fair. And when people perceive you as being fair, they have greater respect for you—as a person and as a leader.

Be a follower, when it's appropriate

Yes, effective leaders know when to follow! Here's the new reality: The ever-expanding pool of human knowledge means that no one can be an expert at everything. So … the wise leader will know when to listen to knowledgeable team members and follow their lead in areas where the team member's knowledge, skill or expertise gives them a better grasp of the situation. This is an application of the "listen and learn" principle that we just presented, but it's especially important when a leader needs to know what is going on "out there" at the interface between the organization and the client or customer. In such cases, the worker who serves at that important interface is often a valuable source of unique insight, accurate information and fresh ideas. And when your people see you in the learning mode—open to new information and ideas—their respect for you soars.

Give people the benefit of the doubt

It always shows respect when you assume the best of others. And that behavior usually results in others giving you the same respect in return. This mindset is important to demonstrate in every business relationship—toward clients, vendors, peers, higher-ups and … your own subordinates. Assuming the best about people is also most likely to inspire and motivate the best behavior in them. That's human nature—we tend to "live up" to any good reputation that others ascribe to us. Use this simple and subtle (but powerful) way to acquire respect from everyone you encounter, especially your own team members.

✓ ACTION STEP

Do you already follow the five practices for earning respect that we've introduced: Treating others with respect, acting with integrity, listening, appropriate following and giving the benefit of the doubt?

Do you know how well you model these behaviors? If not, ask someone you trust— if they know you well, they'll know how well you're doing in those areas.

My behaviors:

1.
2.
3.
4.
5.
6.
7.
8.
9.
10.

CHAPTER 2:

Building trust

Trust enables us to be vulnerable to one another—it means that we can rely on one another for mutual support and also have confidence that we're safe from mutual exploitation or harm. And trust is the secret of high-performing work teams: As trust levels increase, so does productivity. That's right—the more team members trust one another, the more effectively and efficiently they work! Trust is also the secret of high-impact leadership. The more your team members trust you, the more responsive they become to your leadership. To build trust with your team, you must understand where trust comes from.

Trust is a function of consistent behavior. Our ability to trust someone grows as we're able to predict how that person is going to act or react. Think of the opposite scenario: The boss or manager whose behavior is totally unpredictable. When their team members walk through the door for work each day, they never know what they are going to encounter. Is the boss going to be in a good mood or a bad mood? Will I be able to interact effectively with the boss, or will I have to run for cover and stay out of the way? Decide right now that you'll be the kind of leader that your team members can trust. How do you become that kind of leader? Follow these simple guidelines:

Tell the truth

Your integrity—your commitment to clear values—is where you begin. Be committed to the truth and then reinforce it with appropriate behavior. Always tell the truth. Show your team members that you'll always be honest with them—about everything. Set the standard for them, as well—show them that you'll never accept anything other than the truth from them. Be honest and clear about every problem, every situation, every challenge, every behavior, every standard, every expectation and every evaluation. Don't mince words. Say what you mean and mean what you say.

Be accurate

Take truth-telling to the next level—always make sure you have your facts and figures straight. If you don't, then admit it! Be willing to tell your people when you don't know or don't have all the answers. If you try to fake it, they'll know. But if you level with them, they'll respect you for your honesty and vulnerability. And they'll trust you as a leader.

Admit your mistakes …

No one is perfect. Everyone makes mistakes. This is a reality of human nature. Perfection is not a requirement for leadership, but honesty is—when you do make a mistake, be willing to admit it. Cowards try to shift the blame onto others. Leaders are willing to take responsibility. Be a leader. Your honesty in this will earn your team's trust. In fact, you'll find that they will be more willing to trust you with *their* mistakes. And that will make you even more effective as their leader.

… but not your team members'

Never throw your people under the bus. As a team leader, be willing to take responsibility for the failure of your team and your team members. Don't use your team members' mistakes as excuses to shift blame or dodge responsibility. When it comes to ultimate responsibility for the work of your team, the buck stops with you. Anything less will lose the respect of your team (and your boss!). Here's an extreme example of failure to accept responsibility: I knew of a manager who habitually blamed his own mistakes on his team members. How much respect do you think his people had for him?

Keep your promises

In some circles, this is abbreviated: DWYSYWD (Do What You Say You Will Do). Demonstrate follow-through to your team—when you say you are going to do something, do it. This not only earns their respect, it builds their trust. It does something else that is very powerful: It establishes a firm model for their expected behavior as team members. It's the best thing you can do as a leader to teach them to exercise follow-through in their own work and assignments.

No hidden agendas

You must be clear, open and honest about your intentions. Any hint of subversive activity or motive on your part will erode or destroy trust. Indeed, even a personal agenda on your part may actually be accepted and even supported by your team provided you are open about it (e.g., "My personal goal is to advance in this organization and be promoted"). This, too, you can use to model positive team dynamics to your people. After all, the key to real motivation is to find ways to support the personal agendas of your team members—their dreams, goals, aspirations and interests. A powerful key to winning as a team is to enable each team member to win in their own way. The key: Keep everything out in the open and on the table.

No hiding

Be open about your own behavior. Don't try to hide your activities or cover them up with a bogus explanation or false pretense. Your team members will spot your deceit in a moment—and it will earn you their immediate contempt.

No favoritism

Surveys in the workplace show that workers place a high value on fairness. As a leader, you must be willing to enforce standards of performance and excellence consistently among team members—including yourself. Once again, your behavior is the basis for influential modeling. When you are willing to accept the same standards for yourself as you apply to any other team member, you send a strong message to your team—we take these standards seriously.

No deviation

Here is the challenge you face as a leader: You are always "on stage." You are always under the scrutiny of your team. They will be constantly observing your behavior and making personal assessments as a result. Take advantage of this and use it as an opportunity to build strong bridges of trust and support with them. Here's the good news about this challenge: The more consistently you behave, the faster and more strongly you can build trust with your team. When your people learn that you are a person of integrity, honesty, openness, reliability and consistency, they will trust you with their work, their support, their success, their future and themselves.

Up close and personal

General Norman Schwarzkopf has been called "The Hero of Desert Storm" because of the leadership he gave to this incredibly challenging but remarkably successful military initiative. He inspired unusual loyalty, support and respect among his staff. We can understand why that was so when we learn about his own leadership principles:

- Principle #3: Let people know where you stand
- Principle #9: Never lie … ever
- Principle #11: Do what's right

✓ Action step

What are the principles that guide *your* leadership? Have you ever taken time to think about them, let alone write them down or talk about them with your team? Start today! Set aside some time to jot down a few of the "non-negotiables" that guide you in your leadership.

My leadership principles:

1.
2.
3.
4.
5.
6.
7.
8.
9.
10.

CHAPTER 3:

Communicating compassion

Recent studies in the workplace have surfaced an important quality of effective leaders: The ability to hold in tension and balance a commitment to both the work and the worker. In other words, effective leaders aren't just passionate about their mission and their work—they have care and concern for their people as well. Effective leaders tune in to the needs of their team members. They understand that people aren't machines or robots—they have real concerns, worries, pressures, apprehensions, desires and dreams. They know that people have lives outside of work—where any number of issues can affect their performance, availability or energy. Effective leaders are able to understand and empathize—and offer tangible support, encouragement, comfort and assurance. Maybe you've heard this principle before: People don't care how much you know until they know how much you care. How do you communicate genuine concern and compassion for people? Use words that S.A.V.E.:

<u>S</u>upport

Use words that *support*. Words that support sound like this:

- Call me if you have any questions.
- Let me know if you run into any obstacles or setbacks.
- Holler if you need help.
- Send up a flare if you run into any problems.
- I've lined up Dave in accounting to help you with this assignment.

Why is support important? Why does expressing and showing support inspire team members to follow you? Because no one wants to feel that they are out there doing their job all on their own—with no support, no safety net, no one to go to for help. When you send the strong message to your team that you are their ultimate back-up, it tells them that you *care*. And it gets that message across better than any greeting card because it reinforces your concern by promising real, tangible *presence* and *resources* to ensure their success. But don't forget the lesson of the previous chapter—if you promise support, you must be sure to *follow through* with appropriate behavior when the time comes.

<u>A</u>ffirm

Words that affirm sound like this:

- You're doing a great job!
- I'm proud to be working with you!
- Your work is top-notch!

- You're a great addition to our team!
- Your last assignment was a great success!

Affirmation draws people to your leadership like a powerful magnet—because people like to be around other people who make them feel good about themselves! Unfortunately, many bosses and managers have not learned how powerful simple affirmation can be in the workplace. Instead, they have adopted the philosophy of "management by exception." Their approach to managing their people is to remain silent until there is a mistake to correct. Then they speak. Then they communicate. Maybe you have worked for someone like this: Every time they uttered the words "I need to talk to you," it was accompanied by correction or criticism. Workers hate this style of management! If you become an affirming boss, you'll stand head-and-shoulders above the vast crowd of mediocre supervisors who focus only on criticism and fault-finding.

<u>V</u>alidate

What do words of validation sound like? Here is an effective expression of validation:

- I think if I were in your situation, I'd probably feel the same way.

Validation is a way of saying, "I understand your point of view and the emotions you're feeling as a result." Validation does not necessarily mean, "I agree with your point of view and your feelings." Validation merely means: "If I adopted the same point of view that you have, I would probably feel the same feelings that you are feeling." Invalidation is the opposite. It's one of the biggest mistakes we make in interpersonal communication. Here are some examples of invalidating statements:

- You shouldn't be upset about this!
- You shouldn't be angry!
- Why are you upset about this? This is nothing!
- Why are you making such a big deal about this? This is a small thing!
- This is not an important issue—you shouldn't be so concerned about it!

Which approach do you think is most helpful in building bridges of understanding? Think about your own experiences. When you try to calm an angry person by telling them "You shouldn't be mad about this," what effect does it have? Does their anger lessen or increase? The answer is obvious, so it's all the more amazing that most people instinctively make invalidating statements when confronted with anger. Why is that? Maybe it's because invalidating statements are our attempt to make others understand our point of view. Skilled leaders know that the best way to build understanding in a tense situation is to take the first step in attempting to understand the other person's point of view. This is the epitome of compassion. This simple approach makes it easier for the other person to reciprocate and try to understand *our* point of view in return. Next time you are confronted with strong emotion from a member of your team, remember these simple words of validation: *I think if I were in your situation, I'd probably feel the same way.*

Encourage

Words that *encourage* are expressions that literally "put courage into" people. Here are some examples:

- You're doing fine—hang in there!
- Don't give up—you're doing a great job!
- Don't let this get you down—you're doing fine!
- This is just a bump in the road—don't let it get you down!

Encouragement is the emotional antidote to the various sources of discouragement in the workplace: Stress, worry, apprehension, fear, failure, self-doubt, pessimism, negativity and burnout. Words of encouragement lift people up when they're feeling down. Encouragement from a leader sends the message to team members: *You can do it— I believe in you!*

Finally, true compassion for people always involves more than just words—true compassion moves us to *action*. So the final test of your compassion will be whether you are willing to take appropriate action to help solve problems, remove obstacles and provide support—so team members will be able to be effective in their work. When faced with the needs of your team members, always ask yourself: *What can I do to address this issue? How can I help? What steps can I take that will help this person continue to serve effectively on the team?*

UP CLOSE AND PERSONAL

When I was fresh out of graduate school, I took a lowly part-time internship position that gave me some great experience but not a lot of salary. I took a second job to make up the difference—the internship was only a year long, and I figured I could make it work. Our second daughter was just a few months old at the time, so my wife stayed home with the little ones while I worked. It turned out to be one of the most difficult times in our life! I was gone all the time, and the "part-time" internship kept demanding more and more of my time.

Out of frustration, my wife went to the boss to plead our case (I don't recommend that approach, by the way, but we were young, I was overwhelmed and my wife was desperate!) To his credit, the boss understood our predicament and really cared about what was happening to us. He found a way to fund the internship as a full-time position with an appropriate salary. He believed in me enough and cared about me enough to find a way to help me learn, develop and grow as a leader without putting destructive stress on my wife and family.

Is it any wonder that this guy is in my Leadership Hall of Fame?

✓ ACTION STEP

Plan appropriate words that S.A.V.E. for each of your team members.

Here's a suggestion: Write down each team member's name. Then list any of the words that S.A.V.E. that are appropriate for that team member and their particular situation. Take a few moments to actually write down what you plan to say to your team member.

Team member:	Words that S.A.V.E.:
1.	
2.	
3.	
4.	
5.	
6.	
7.	
8.	
9.	
10.	

If you like, share these with a trusted colleague who is willing to give you some feedback. Make a commitment to yourself to share these statements in the week that follows.

CHAPTER 4:

Demonstrating competence

It's human nature—we're much more likely to respect people who we believe to have knowledge, skills or experience that we don't. You can use this to reinforce your leadership—you can acquire respect by demonstrating expertise and competence. Start by demonstrating expertise in the arena of your team's work. For example, if you supervise a team of accountants, you should demonstrate skill and expertise in accounting. But don't stop there …

- Become an expert on your organization—its structure, policies and people
- Gain an understanding of your organization in a way that will enable you to be more effective and help your team become more effective
- Learn who the decision-makers are
- Build rapport with key players in other departments—people whose work affects your success and the success of your team
- Know the rules of the organization better than anyone else, so you can use them to your advantage
- Make sure you have a clear grasp of the vision and values of your organization— what drives the goals and decisions of its leaders

Now learn the business. Learn how your organization conducts its business and succeeds in the marketplace. Find out how it generates profitability or delivers successful service to its clients and customers. Your goal is to understand exactly how your team fits into the bigger picture of the organization—how your team contributes to the vision of the organization and how your team can operate in alignment with the values of the organization. Take this learning to the next level and learn the industry. See the big picture of where your organization fits in the marketplace—where it's positioned with regard to chief competitors and key consumers. This will equip you to lead your team with greater insight and wider perspective, and it will gain you the respect of your people.

Now learn how to be a better leader, manager and boss. Research in the workplace shows that workers really enjoy working for a manager who knows how to manage well. That simple revelation is a key to building influence among your team members. Use every resource at your disposal to acquire good leadership skills—take advantage of training opportunities, seek advice from experienced colleagues, recruit a mentor and build a library of materials that will guide your development and shorten your learning curve. When you demonstrate wise and effective leadership, your team members will respect you, trust you and support you.

✓ ACTION STEP

Use the suggestions in the last paragraph above to make a "to-do" list for yourself. Add any items you feel are appropriate or helpful to your situation. Set goals to accomplish each item (make sure you attach a deadline or time line to each goal). Your list might look something like this:

To do:	Deadline:
1. Recruit a mentor	By the end of this year
2. Add one new book or audio resource to my management skills library	This quarter
3. Register for the next management training class offered	By the end of this month
4. Identify and recruit a colleague I can use for idea sharing and feedback	THIS WEEK
5.	
6.	
7.	
8.	
9.	
10.	

CHAPTER 5:

Engaging emotions

Someone has said that you can *manage* resources, but you must *lead* people. Even if we concede that people need management too, we must also recognize that people are not the same as the other resources that managers must manage. People have minds and emotions. Effective leaders know how to tap into the uniquely human potential of their team members—for thinking, feeling and doing.

The challenge is that people are unique—they respond differently to circumstances, stressors and other people. To engage each person emotionally, a leader must understand how each person is most likely to be engaged—which means understanding which emotions trigger or motivate each person to action. This will require effective team leaders to know their people well—to know which emotions will move each of their team members to action. To motivate your team member, which emotion will you have to engage?

Will it be their feeling of *pride?*

- Pride from beating the competition
- Pride in great achievement
- Pride from gaining prominence or notoriety
- Pride in receiving affirmation from someone they respect or admire

What about their feeling of *loyalty?*

- Loyalty to a leader they admire and respect
- Loyalty to team members whose friendship and admiration they value
- Loyalty to an organization that has employed, supported and provided for them
- Loyalty to a family they love and are committed to supporting

Do you engage their feelings of *satisfaction?*

- Satisfaction from mastering a difficult skill
- Satisfaction from overcoming a challenging obstacle
- Satisfaction from solving a tough problem
- Satisfaction from conquering a daunting challenge

Are they more likely to respond to feelings of *fulfillment?*

- Fulfillment from learning
- Fulfillment from personal growth
- Fulfillment from professional development
- Fulfillment from advancement and promotion
- Fulfillment from achieving an important goal or experiencing a major milestone

Will they respond to the simple feeling of *joy?*

- Joy in expressing their gifts and talents
- Joy of friendship and camaraderie
- Joy of creating an excellent product or outcome
- Joy of serving people well

Emotions are at the center of personal motivation—they provide the energy and the drive behind human will and behavior. When you trigger emotions in your team members, you are tapping into incredible motivational power. Use this power to help your team members become more effective. But do your homework—get to know your people well enough to be able to appeal to each person's unique emotional triggers.

Up close and personal

Most company presidents and CEOs I have met are strong, hard-driving, determined leaders. One chief executive I reported to was particularly competitive. In fact, competition was one of his very strong emotional triggers. If I wanted to sell him on my idea, all I had to do was tell him "No one else is doing this in our industry—we'll be on top of the heap if we do this," and he was instantly engaged. Was this effective motivational skill on my part or just mere manipulation?

Trust me, this particular leader was a very independent thinker—ultimately, no one could really manipulate him. My approach was nothing more than effective, emotionally connected communication.

✓ Action step

List each of your team members and the emotional triggers that are most likely to move them to action. Next time you make an assignment or ask for their commitment to a project, craft statements and appeals that are specific to each team member's emotional triggers.

If you can't identify your team members' emotional triggers, then plan some one-on-one time with them to discuss this issue. You can also use this approach: Craft a team-building event around a group discussion of this issue, and encourage each team member to reflect on their emotional triggers and share them with the rest of the team.

Team member:	Trigger:
1.	
2.	
3.	
4.	
5.	
6.	
7.	

CHAPTER 6:

Forging a vision

Vision is central to leadership. It's what sets leaders apart from managers. Effective managers focus on what exists now: The status quo. They make sure that people, processes and resources are deployed effectively and managed efficiently. Leaders focus on what doesn't exist *yet:* The future. Leaders have the ability to know when (and how) the status quo itself must be changed, discarded or replaced. They are driven by an energy to create a new status quo—a better status quo. This is the essence of vision: A preferred future state. Many leaders have an instinct regarding this drive to create a better future—they "see" the future intuitively in their thoughts and imagination. For them, it's a foregone conclusion— an assumption that is not subject to debate or analysis. Effective team leaders are able to express vision clearly and help their people develop ownership of a team vision that creates a dynamic focus for team direction, energy and work. It's this vision—this potential for a better future—that inspires team members to join with their leader and work together to make the dream a reality, to see their combined efforts make a difference, to make the world a better place!

But there are two vital imperatives here: First, the team's vision must be in alignment with the vision and values of the organization—it must serve the purposes of the organization in which the team exists and works. Second, you must not simply impose your vision on your team—they must have an opportunity to forge this vision with you. Otherwise, they will lack ownership and have little personal commitment to the vision. So … where do you begin?

Begin with the vision and values of the organization. Start with a clear understanding of what is driving the organization you serve. It might be customer service, or quality manufacturing, or the health and safety of clients and customers, or market share, or industry recognition, or maybe just plain profitability. Whatever it is, your team vision must serve the organization's vision by contributing to it in a tangible way. So start with a statement of your organization's vision and then build your team vision statement around it. Here's what that might look like for various kinds of organizations and teams …

Heavy equipment manufacturing:

Organizational vision—to be recognized by customers as the preferred supplier in all markets we serve

Service Division team vision—to service and repair our equipment better, faster and more safely than any other source available to our customers

Health services:

Organizational vision—to offer quality care that exceeds patients' expectations in a caring, convenient, cost-effective and accessible manner

Medical Records team vision—to maintain accurate, complete and accessible records for our patients in a way that provides efficient, safe and responsive service to physicians, patients and insurance providers

Financial services:

Organizational vision—to be the most useful and ethical financial services firm in the world

IT Department team vision—provide timely and responsive IT support to every department and individual in our company to enable high productivity and rapid, accurate customer service

Home construction:

Organizational vision—to offer quality housing, excellent value and memorable service to all home buyers and prospective home buyers

Engineering team vision—provide timely, high-quality engineering consulting services that save project time, lower costs and reduce company and customer liability

Restaurant:

Organizational vision—provide patrons with the freshest, highest-quality food available and present each meal with friendly service in a sparkling clean environment

Human Resources Department team vision—give every leader in the organization the tools they need to effectively manage, support, evaluate and train their people—so as to raise productivity, lower turnover, increase employee satisfaction and deliver superior, friendly service to customers.

UP CLOSE AND PERSONAL

In one of my seminars, I had a student who worked for the city where the workshop was located. Before the seminar actually began, I had a chance to talk with him about his work and his role. I wanted to know what he did for the city, so I asked him directly: *What is your focus there?* He could have answered any number of ways. He could have said, "I manage two shifts of a hundred workers with a fleet of trucks and a multi-million dollar budget" or something of that nature. Instead, he just smiled and said two words: *"Clean streets."* That's what I call "clear vision."

Don't make vision more complicated than it needs to be. Keep it as simple and as tangible as possible. But be specific. Don't confuse your team with meaningless generalities—make sure they have a solid target for everything they do.

✓ ACTION STEP

Use these examples to help you and your team craft a clear team vision statement. You also can use and adapt the following basic "template" to guide your thinking and writing:

We're creating, designing, building …

[describe the PROCESS or PRODUCT you are offering through your team's work]

In such a way …

[describe your METHOD of delivering this process or product]

That …

[define the specific EFFECT or RESULTS you hope to achieve]

As measured by …

[describe the BENCHMARKS that will exist if you are successful]

CHAPTER 7:

Gaining support

Effective leaders inspire their teams by building a broad base of support in the organization—a base of support that enhances the effectiveness and success of the team. It begins with gaining the support of higher-ups, especially the team leader's boss. (We'll share more ideas about that important relationship in later chapters!) Additionally, effective team leaders build mutually supportive relationships with key players in other departments and divisions in the organization—people whose work contributes to the success of the team, even though the team leader has no formal authority over them. These are internal business alliances.

As you read this, certain people in your organization may come to mind—people whose work is essential to your success but who report to another manager in the organization. When you need them to perform, you can't harangue them or threaten them. That doesn't work. Your only recourse is to build a relationship with them based on rapport and mutual support. In other words, you do what you can to enable them to be effective; you give them what they need to succeed, so they will reciprocate and help you in return. This requires you to think beyond the bureaucratic boundaries that separate different teams in an organization and adopt a cooperative and collaborative mindset. It means conforming to the processes and procedures that other departments (and leaders) require, so you can earn their enthusiastic appreciation and support. It also means showing consideration to your colleagues and letting go of the need to be an outsider or "lone wolf." In return, you ultimately gain respect, support and help—not just from your associates, but from your team members as well. You also provide a model for positive organizational behavior to your team—you show them how to cooperate and collaborate as a team. And you demonstrate the benefits that result.

If you need help identifying the key internal business alliances for you and your team and how best to support those alliances, just sit down with paper and pencil and do some thoughtful analysis. Use these questions to guide your thinking:

- Who do we depend on in other departments in order to get our own work done?
- What processes, procedures, forms, permissions or authorizations are we routinely required to use in our work, and who are they connected to in our organization?

Once you've identified these key individuals, go to them and find out how you can cooperate and collaborate with them. Find out what they need from you. The following questions are good ones to ask to learn how to give tangible support to these important co-workers:

- What do you need from me in order to do your work?
- What can I do that will enable you to do your work more easily, efficiently or effectively?
- What drives you crazy—the things that make it more difficult for you to do your work?
- What are realistic deadlines for you in completing your work?
- What kind of lead time do you need or prefer in order to get your work done effectively?

If you are willing to be a good listener, you'll doubtless learn some very specific ways you can help these key people be more effective. If you are willing to be a *humble leader* and exercise some flexibility and cooperation, you'll reap valuable rewards in gaining the support you need to lead your own team to greater effectiveness and impact.

UP CLOSE AND PERSONAL

One organization I worked with had a key administrative support person who controlled access to key resources in the organization, including facilities—an essential element for the success of my leadership training programs there. (My work lived or died depending on the availability of space to conduct my training courses and workshops.) This particular support person had a reputation for being "tough" and difficult to work with or please. Many people in the organization trod lightly around her, afraid of ending up on her wrong side and losing her active support.

When I joined the staff, I had a brief conversation with her about facility scheduling. I asked her, "What do you need from me in order to make this process as simple and as easy as possible for you?" After a long diatribe about the multitude of problems she faced because of irresponsible staff members, she outlined her preferences for me. From that moment on, collaboration with her was a walk in the park—I became one of her best in-house "clients" by simply meeting her basic requests for an accurate scheduling form and a reasonable lead time. I always had the rooms I needed.

✓ ACTION STEP

Set aside time to sit down with pencil and paper and list the key business alliances you need to build in order to succeed as a team leader in your organization. You can do this alone, or you can do this with your team. Use the questions in this chapter to guide your thinking.

Key alliances:	Key support:
1.	
2.	
3.	
4.	
5.	
6.	
7.	
8.	
9.	
10.	
11.	
12.	

For each person you identify, describe the things you can do to support them in their work and add to their effectiveness, productivity or success. Use this list to guide your interactions with each key person. (You may also want to share this list with your team to help them understand their role in supporting these important relationships!)

PART II:

Motivate—Igniting Your Team's Personal Passion

Here's the tough truth about motivation: You can't really motivate anyone! Vast research has demonstrated that the only motivation that really moves people comes from within. No one can come along and wave a magic wand that will create, transfer or infuse motivation into a person. It just doesn't work that way. To master the fine art of motivation, you'll have to do the hard work of understanding people—in particular, understanding *your* people.

You can start by understanding yourself better. What do you value in your life? What matters to you? What are you interested in? What do you enjoy most about your work? What do you enjoy least? What kind of working relationship do you prefer with your boss? How do you prefer being recognized for good work? What do you hope to accomplish through your work? Why do you do the things that you do? The answers to these questions reveal a lot about what motivates you—they reveal the real reasons why you show up every day at work and give your best effort.

Your team members have their own motivations just as you do—they have their own answers to the same questions. Their answers will help you understand how to connect their very individual and personal motivations to your team's vision and team's work. When you help them make that connection, you are unleashing their personal passion—a powerful energy that fuels their best efforts and leads to their very best work.

Each chapter in this section will give you a fresh approach for making that all-important connection— the keys to fanning the flames of each team member's internal fire of motivation!

CHAPTER 8:

Identifying common values and interests for alignment and impact

Entrepreneur Mary Kay Ash made a fortune by creating a company that appealed to women who valued success and had an interest in achievement. It was a company that was born out of her own frustration with the artificial limits that American corporations placed on the success and achievement of women. This prejudicial corporate culture came to be known as the "glass ceiling" in American businesses. A much more candid and honest version of this euphemism was recently offered by a female executive who was able to achieve success despite this prejudice against women in business. She explained, "There really isn't a glass ceiling in American corporations, just a very thick layer of men." Mary Kay Ash decided to create a different kind of company—one that would not artificially limit the success and achievement of women. The business she created had great appeal among women who shared the same value of success and had the same interest in achievement. She enjoyed immense success because she gave these women a way to experience the success they valued and pursue the interest they had in personal achievement.

You can do what Mary Kay Ash did. You can succeed by unleashing the motivation that already exists within each of your team members. You can do this by showing your team members how to experience what they value and pursue what interests them by helping the team succeed and achieve its goals. To do this, you must first identify the values and interests of your team members. Then you must connect those values and interests with the vision and goals of your team. Use Mary Kay Cosmetics as a model. Women who affiliate with this company are known for their passion to succeed and achieve. The leaders and managers of Mary Kay Cosmetics don't try to instill this passion in company representatives; they merely provide opportunities for women who already have this value and interest to connect that passion with the company vision and goals.

Now it's your turn. Help your team members to connect their values and interests to the vision and goals of your team. You begin this process by identifying their individual values and interests. What are they? Use the list below to stimulate your thinking, but don't limit yourself to the list. Above all, don't be hesitant to actually talk to your team members and ask them about their values.

VALUES people hold ...

Excellence	Success
Prominence	Friendship/community
Service	Truth
Honesty	Accuracy
Personal/professional growth	Contribution
Creativity	Synergy
Happiness	Significance

Finally, keep in mind that "interests" is a broad category that includes hobbies and avocations. Some of your team members may reserve their greatest passion for a hobby they pursue outside the workplace during personal time. That's OK—if you can show them how their success at work will provide the financial means to pursue their hobby, then you have helped them make an important connection that will motivate them to perform on the job.

INTERESTS people have ...

Achievement	Advancement
Acceptance	Approval
Challenge	Learning
Impact	Affiliation
Satisfaction	Job security

Up close and personal

My own experience in organizations is another example. One of my strong personal values is excellence. I have always had a passion to excel in everything that I do—I abhor mediocrity in myself, especially in areas where I have the skill and expertise to perform with excellence. I love the challenge of performing at my best, and I have always wanted to be associated with other high-performers. I always wanted to be in the company of eagles, not surrounded by turkeys! As a result, I have always been attracted to organizations (and teams) that shared the same value of excellence. If you were managing me, you could always ignite my fire of passion by tapping into that value. All you had to do was say to me: We need your help with this, because we want to do this with the very highest quality possible! Whenever I heard those words, I was always on board with the program and ready to give my best.

✓ Action step

Set aside time to sit down with pencil and paper and list your team members and the values and interests that each of them embrace. Then think about ways you can connect those values and interests with the vision and goals of your team. Here's an example:

Bob values achievement and has an interest in promotion and advancement. Show Bob how his contribution to the success of the team will give him tangible achievements he can list on his résumé and help him gain the visibility with higher-ups that he needs in order to get promoted. Show him how his work on the team will also give him opportunity to acquire and develop the skills and experience that will make him more promotable.

Team member:	Values/interests:
1.	
2.	
3.	
4.	
5.	

CHAPTER 9:

Connecting individual motivation with team vision

Are you still trying to motivate your team members? Stop. It's an exercise in futility. The secret is to realize that your people are already motivated. Your real task as a leader is to identify their motivations and figure out how to connect those motivations with your team vision. Let me give you an illustration that may help you to grasp this concept.

I was training a group of managers in this very subject when one of them complained, "I don't have any problems motivating my team at work—they're all very motivated sales people, with plenty of energy and passion to succeed. The person I have trouble motivating is my teenage son." I asked this frustrated father to help me understand exactly what he was talking about. He told me, "My son isn't motivated about anything!" "Really?" I asked, "Why do you say that?" The father explained, "He's not motivated to clean up his room, do his homework or get good grades. He's just not motivated!" I assured this frustrated father that his son was not without motivation. I explained, "Give me five minutes with your son, and I'll discover what is motivating him. Now … it may not be what *you* would like to be motivating him, but I assure you that he is motivated by something. It might be skateboards, or surfboards, or snowboards, or even members of the opposite gender on skateboards, surfboards or snowboards. But he is definitely motivated by something. Your job as a father is to discover what is motivating your son, and find a way to connect his motivations with your interests." The father followed my advice and had a serious heart-to-heart conversation with his son. He offered to raise his son's allowance (which would support his son's true interests) in exchange for some accountability with regard to homework and grades.

You must do the same with your team members. You must discover what is motivating them and connect those motivations with your interest in pursuing your team vision and accomplishing your team's goals. So, what is motivating your people? Look over the following list and use it as a starting point to help you identify each team member's inner drive and passion. The list comes from extensive surveys in the workplace, so you're sure to find some key motivations that your team members will identify as their own. Keep in mind that this is only the first step—your work will not be complete until you help each team member connect their motivations with your team vision and goals.

Key motivations in the workplace

Think about how each of the following motivations can be connected with your team vision and goals. Think about what you must do as a manager to be able to respond appropriately to each of these motivators. This is some of the most challenging work you must do as a leader. Be creative. Think outside the box. Get help—suggestions and ideas—from other managers. Start with the suggestions below, but don't limit yourself to them!

Recognition. Keep track of individual performance, so you can recognize and reward high-performing team members. Provide appropriate rewards and recognition for high performance (this will be expanded on in the next chapter). Don't ignore the good work of team members who perform "behind the scenes"—be sure to recognize their unique contributions and achievements.

Meaningful or significant work. Help team members see how their work impacts the organization and its clients in meaningful ways. Highlight those aspects of the organizational vision that impact the customers *and* the community in ways that team members consider meaningful or significant (e.g., the health and safety of our clients, the well-being of the community, the improvement of the environment, the enrichment of our customer's lives, etc.). Share information about how the organization is actually achieving this vision through its work, its special projects or its charitable contributions. Share customer praises with your team, so they can hear from actual clients how their work has had a positive impact. Give team members an opportunity to interact directly with clients or customers to see for themselves how their work is having a positive effect.

A role that really matters. Show your team members why their work is important to the team and how it has a significant impact on the team's effectiveness and on the organization's ultimate success. Help them understand the hardship their absence would create for the team. Affirm their contributions with verbal references, both privately and publicly. Have your boss write a note of recognition or appreciation that affirms the importance of their contribution. Assign team members to task forces that are commissioned with important projects within the organization.

Freedom and independence in working conditions. Don't micromanage your team members! When you give them an assignment, be clear about the outcomes you want, the control you're giving them and the communication "checkpoints" you'll establish in order to monitor progress. Then turn them loose on the assignment! Give them the freedom to complete the task in their own way as long as they meet the other requirements (e.g., outcomes and deadlines). Allow them some flexibility in their work schedule, if you can. Some team members will also benefit from the freedom to have a certain amount of isolation in their work in order to eliminate interruptions, focus on their assignment and work with higher productivity.

Challenging work or assignments. Keep a sharp eye on the growth and development of your team members. As they master their work, they will be ready for greater challenges. Be prepared to expand their responsibilities or assign special projects that will provide the challenge they seek. Use team members as mentors. Partner experienced team members with new hires—to show them the ropes, help them adjust to their new roles and provide a trusted source that can answer their questions and smooth their transition into the organization and the team.

Personal growth and development/professional growth and development. Show team members that you are willing to help them in their desire for growth and development. Find opportunities for team members to take advantage of formal training experiences—within the organization or with classes or seminars offered by outside sources. Cover the expense of training opportunities or at least underwrite them. Make yourself available to coach your team members—to help them acquire or refine specific skills. Help team members identify and recruit mentors within the organization or within a broader professional network. Provide resources for self-study and development: Books, manuals, audio media and on-line sources. Partner with local educational institutions to provide certifications or continuing education credits.

Career advancement. Help your team members identify "career paths" within your organization. Make appropriate recommendations for their advancement and promotion. Be available to coach them—to help them develop specific skills that will aid in their promotion (e.g., budgeting and finance, presentation, interpersonal skills, strategic planning, organization, management and leadership). Help them gain visibility with higher-ups in the organization. Give them assignments that will expand their skills and also give higher-ups an opportunity to see them succeed. Pave the way for their advancement by letting your boss know what you are trying to do. Gain support for your efforts from higher-ups in the organization. Help team members identify positions within the organization that they can apply for, and help them prepare for the interview and screening processes involved.

Job security. Help team members commit to the kind of job success that will ensure greater job security. Help them identify and embrace the personal qualities that add value to any worker in your organization (e.g., positive attitude, enthusiasm, reliability, flexibility, even temper, openness, willingness to learn, etc.). Provide cross-training. Help them discover job roles and assignments that have longevity in the business of the organization.

Friendships in the workplace. More and more people are spending more and more time at work. Consequently, working relationships have become the chief source of socialization and friendship for many. You can tap into this very special need with just a few simple initiatives. Create times within the workday when socialization is appropriate and encouraged. That can take the form of a monthly birthday celebration in the break room, a Monday afternoon coffee break or a Friday (or monthly) potluck lunch. Plan social events for the team outside the workplace and outside normal working hours (e.g., attendance at local athletic events, tailgating, picnics or barbecues, holiday celebrations, etc.). Encourage special activities that invite connection and mutual support or appreciation, like Secret Santas or the like. Encourage team participation in organization-wide athletic leagues or special-interest groups. Or try participation *as a team* in community-based leagues. You can also consider encouraging your team to participate in community-based charitable events and special projects. As you participate together as a team, the opportunity creates a bonding experience that draws team members closer together through shared history.

Having a "say" in decisions, policies, plans and goals. Some team members are looking for shared leadership at the team level. You can begin this process by simply asking for their input and ideas. Use the magic phrase, "What do *you* think?" Be prepared to listen authentically and give team members your genuine attention and focus. Respond appropriately to their ideas with experimentation and reward. Include them in problem solving and decision making. Use the liberal application of consultative decision making. That means you make the final decision, but you encourage your team members' input, ideas, suggestions and recommendations in order to help you make a better decision—just be sure they understand up front that it isn't going to be a consensus decision. Include your team in strategic planning whenever possible. Set aside special times when the team can gather for special problem solving or goal setting. Of course, you want your team members to have agreement and buy-in for all your team goals. The best way to achieve that is to allow them to participate in *setting* those goals—elicit their ideas at the outset, and you'll gain their commitment for the work required to make those goals a reality. Your team members will also feel more like "insiders" who matter when you treat them like shareholders in the organization by sharing important information with them. So keep them informed about events in the organization—even what is happening in other departments. Feed them news about the organization's successes and developments, including how it's performing in the marketplace. And keep them abreast of new developments in the *industry*—any information that is relevant to the organization and its business.

✓ ACTION STEP

List your team members and their top two or three motivations. If you are having difficulty doing this, copy the list provided and have your team members rank them in order of importance to them, or have them rate each on a scale of one to ten with regard to their importance (e.g., if recognition is an important motivator for a team member, they would rate it with an eight, nine or even ten if recognition is their *primary* motivator). This approach might seem a bit mechanical or impersonal, but if it reveals accurate information, it will help you to establish meaningful work relationships with your team members—which is as personal as it is significant!

Team member:

RATE from 1 to 10 ...

☐ Recognition		☐ Meaningful work
☐ Role		☐ Freedom
☐ Challenges		☐ Personal/professional growth
☐ Advancement		☐ Job security
☐ Friendships		☐ Having a "say" in decisions

Now determine how to link each motivation with your team vision and goals. Use the suggestions provided in this chapter (but don't limit yourself to them) and be sure to *individualize them* for each team member.

CHAPTER 10:

Crafting jobs that engage workers and maximize their strengths

What is the ideal match for a worker and their job?

Is it a good idea to assign a job that is much "bigger" than the person—a job that is much greater than their skills or experience? That situation creates frustration for a worker and leads to anger, discouragement and defeat. Is it a good idea to assign a job that is "smaller" than the person—a job for which the worker is easily overqualified? That situation often creates frustration of another kind—boredom and disengagement. Then, does it make sense to match the job perfectly with the worker's skill and experience? That situation may be a happy one at first, but it quickly evolves into the "overqualification" scenario, in which a worker is often bored—lacking interest or challenge. Here's the ideal: Most workers are happiest when faced with a job that is slightly "bigger" than they are—a job that provides enough challenge to be interesting, but not so much challenge that it's overwhelming and defeating. This raises an obvious question: How well-matched are your team members with regard to their jobs and their work assignments?

This question is not an easy one to answer, because your team members are "moving targets" who don't stand still. They are constantly growing and changing as they learn and develop. Consequently, the challenge they face today quickly becomes another lesson they have mastered. That's good news in the sense that they are continually growing in skill, self-confidence and their capacity for impact on the team. But it's bad news in the sense that that they will, over time, outgrow their current job and work assignments and face potential boredom and disengagement. What's a team leader to do?

Your job is to continually re-craft each team member's job and work assignments in order to keep providing interesting challenge and engagement for your team. Maybe that's why every job description has that special clause in it—"And other work as assigned by supervisor." That is the "elastic" clause you'll need to invoke in order to keep every team member engaged, interested, challenged and motivated. The challenge for you as a team leader is two-fold: First, discerning when team members are ready for a new challenge; and second, finding ways to supply that challenge.

There are a number of signs that will help you determine if team members are well-matched with their assignments: A healthy pace of work activity on the job; a full (but not destructive) workload; occasional, but not *continual,* calls for help and support; openness to coaching and learning; and active engagement with a strong personal focus on the work itself. But why guess about this? A much better approach is to simply ask. Talk to your team members and find out for certain how they are doing. Simple questions will help you quickly gain a grasp of the situation:

- How are you doing in your job?
- Is your work too overwhelming for you right now?
- Is your job becoming fairly routine?
- Are you ready for a new challenge?
- Would you be interested in a new assignment?

It will also help you to have a frank conversation with them about their career goals and personal aspirations. If you know where your people are headed, you are in a much better position to know what you can do to help them get there. And you have many more tools at your disposal than you might think. Consider the following ways you can expand job descriptions or broaden work assignments:

- Advancement to a "lead" position
- Appropriate promotion to a higher level
- Delegating appropriate aspects of your own work
- Involving team members in key functions of your work and responsibilities (e.g., "you're going to help me craft next year's budget proposal")
- Giving them leadership responsibility for certain team tasks or projects
- Creating opportunities for cross-training or job rotation
- Assigning team members to serve on interdepartmental teams, projects, committees or ad hoc groups
- Giving assignments that actually *require* personal or professional development
- Helping team members find and recruit mentors

All of these are simple ways that you can add more challenge and growth for your team members. But don't stop there. Consider the very nature of their work and how well it fits their strengths and gifts.

The concept of "strengths" or "gifts" has been in consideration in the workplace for many years, but only recently has it received visibility and focused study. Employers want to know more about gifts and strengths because researchers now are associating these with high productivity and high work satisfaction. In other words, when people are working in their area of giftedness, they are as much as 200 percent more productive than when they are not working in the area of their personal gifts. And they are extremely engaged—so much so that workers actually lose track of time because they are so pleasurably involved in their work.

Wouldn't we all want to have a job that we enjoy so much that we actually lose ourselves in the pleasure of doing it? And wouldn't it be a boon to every employer to have their employees working at the 200 percent productivity level? Is such a thing even possible? According to recent studies, it's possible. And the wise team leader will do everything possible to match team members with work assignments that align with each one's unique gifts and strengths. But how does one do that?

It helps to have some idea of what these unique strengths and gifts actually are—what they are based on, what they look like, what type of work they are associated with and what they accomplish. A word of caution is in order here: Human potential is a vastly complex state of affairs, so any attempt to define it or categorize it will always fall far short of the actual reality. No system for understanding human talent, giftedness or aptitude will ever be comprehensive or completely accurate. Nonetheless, there are some basic ways to approach giftedness that can still be of help and service in understanding each person's unique strengths.

You can think in terms of three broad categories of strength or talent: Personal, Conceptual and Mechanical.

Personal strengths include talents associated with work that involve interpersonal relationships: Building friendships, networking, salesmanship, dramatic ability, creative communication (speaking/teaching/training/coaching/advising/mentoring/counseling), organizing and leading teams, mediating and resolving conflict and recruiting.

Mechanical strengths include building, crafting, assembling and creative design; fixing, repairing, adapting, arranging and organizing things; and drawing, painting, sculpting and applying. People with mechanical gifts are hands-on workers who interact physically with their environment.

Conceptual strengths include analyzing, diagnosing and theorizing; seeing connections and understanding systems; formulating vision, goals and strategic plans; organizing concepts, tasks, goals or resources; managing work, resources or details; designing, managing and troubleshooting processes; and creative thinking, writing and composing.

Once again, simple conversations with team members can be of tremendous help in identifying their strengths and gifts. Use the following questions to guide the conversation:

- Describe your best day at work in the last six months.
- Describe your ideal or perfect workday.
- When are you happiest at work?
- What kind of work are you doing when you are happiest at work?
- What kind of work do you enjoy the most?
- What kind of work do you enjoy the least?
- When do you lose yourself in your work?
- What kind of work are you doing when time seems to just fly by?

The more you can craft a team member's work assignments around their strengths and gifts, the more productive they will be and the happier they will be on the job. So use this principle to help your team members become more actively engaged with their work and their jobs.

✓ ACTION STEP

Set aside time to talk with each of your team members. Identify how well-matched they are in their work with regard to appropriate challenge and giftedness. Use the suggested questions to help you with this process. Then create a plan for each of your team members—a plan to help you move them into greater alignment in their work with regard to challenge and giftedness. Keep a list of each team member's gifts and strengths close at hand to use as a reference whenever you are handing out work assignments or assigning jobs and tasks.

Team member:	Gifts/strengths:
1.	
2.	
3.	
4.	
5.	
6.	
7.	
8.	
9.	
10.	
11.	
12.	

CHAPTER 11:

Tailoring unique rewards that affirm and value each individual

Here's an important question for every leader to consider: What is the best way to reward high performance on your team or recognize a worker's contribution to team success? If you know anything about human nature, you'll recognize this immediately as a trick question—our need for *individualized* reward is as unique as our thirst for recognition is universal. Each of us has our own preferences for reward and recognition. The wise and effective team leader will understand this and take it into careful consideration whenever crafting rewards for team members. So what are some key insights that will guide us in this all-important leadership function?

You can start by identifying each member's preferred "language" of reward. Everyone has at least one or two. There are five basic preferences:

1. Physical touch

2. Written or verbal words

3. Gifts

4. Acts of service or appreciation

5. Time and attention

Let's examine them more closely and surface some ideas for using each one appropriately.

1. **Physical touch:** In today's workplace, employees and managers alike must be extremely careful with regard to their behavior, particularly avoiding any hint of bias or sexual harassment. And yet ... in our business-related culture we still retain an understanding of the physical nature of humanity in our colloquialisms about recognition. We still refer to affirmation as a "pat on the back." Is there still a place

for appropriate physical expressions of affirmation in the workplace? I believe that there is. An enthusiastic handshake is still an appropriate expression of affirmation in the culture of business. When it's accompanied by an authentic verbal expression of praise or recognition, it can be a powerfully affirming combination! One might even argue for the appropriateness of a light pat on the back or touch of the shoulder accompanied by the same positive verbal affirmations.

In any case, we always add weight to anything we say when we *embody* our message with physical accompaniments like vocal emphasis, gesture and facial expression. Decide right now that you'll communicate recognition with positive energy and personal enthusiasm—you'll be a much more effective communicator and leader if you do!

2. **Written or spoken words:** There is an unfortunate attitude among many managers today that "my people don't need me to tell them they're doing a good job—they already know if they're doing well." My experience in training thousands of middle managers is quite the opposite—the overwhelming majority want to know if they are hitting the mark and pleasing the boss. How will they know unless the boss says something? Your people are no different. But some of them are more personally impacted by a positive expression that is verbalized or written. So start talking and start writing! Just be sure to follow the rules for effective feedback: Make it timely, specific and genuine. Don't complicate it—keep it simple. You can deliver a verbal word of affirmation anytime and anywhere. You can certainly say something in a team meeting, especially in front of other team members. That has another wonderful advantage—it gives visibility to a team member's performance and presents it as a positive example to the rest of the team. It sends a subtle but very strong message to other team members: If you want the same recognition, do the same thing that this team member did. You also can say something to a team member during normal work—on a job site or in the office—and deliver a positive word of recognition on the spot.

Is it better to say something privately or in a public setting? Certainly, some individuals are uncomfortable being in the spotlight and doubtless prefer a private conversation with the boss. And yet—if it fits the individual—why not do both? Think of the double impact of a private word of affirmation that is repeated in front of the team—most people will enjoy the second helping of affirmation! And don't forget the powerful impact of praising your team members to others in the organization—it's a wonderful way to share credit with deserving people and raise your own credibility in the process. It has an added effect when you praise your people to others in front of them. Your team's success is a strong reflection of your own. And when you praise them, you receive a bit of your own praise indirectly (but without looking self-serving!).

Written recognition can take many forms as well. Sometimes a simple handwritten note from you has enormous value. You might be astonished at the number of people who cherish such expressions—framing them or posting them on the wall or even carrying them around in their purse or wallet. Surely that tells us how rare those expressions are in the workplace, as well as how important they are to certain individuals! Don't forget the possibility of having your boss write a note of commendation for one of your team members. That has an added value of bringing your team's success to the attention of your boss. It's a subtle way you can attract attention to your success without appearing self-serving.

Certificates or printed awards also have tremendous value—especially because we all accept it as appropriate to proudly display such items. And we do proudly display them. They are tangible, visible evidences of our success. Further, don't neglect the power of a few lines of praise published in the organizational or employee newsletter. If you don't consider yourself a writer—practice! Learn a few key phrases that you can use to express recognition effectively. Consider using commercially-prepared greeting cards created for that purpose—sometimes, the humor or professional expression of these cards adds another positive dimension that makes the praise even more memorable. And yes, e-mail messages have value as well, although they may not have quite the same personal quality as a handwritten note.

3. **Gifts:** I'm a great fan of corporate "swag," and I find myself in good company in this regard—many workers enjoy recognition in the form of company merchandise. Coffee mugs, office implements/supplies, key chains, pins, jewelry, baseball caps, t-shirts or other forms of clothing—the variation is endless. Every company's marketing department is usually equipped with various forms of logo-endowed goods that can serve as appropriate gifts of reward or recognition. Some leaders even create point systems that allow their team members to accrue rewarded credits toward the acquisition of various products, including expensive items that they would not be able to afford otherwise.

Gift cards from various sources are also appropriate rewards. As with anything, it's important to match the gift appropriately with the receiver. (This is when it's helpful to know if a worker has a particular hobby or interest that can be matched with a gift card from a store or outlet that will serve their special interest.) Gift certificates also can reward meals at local restaurants, reimburse tickets to movies or special events, provide various personal services and even allow general use that can be used as widely as a typical credit card.

This category can also include special allowances or privileges—a well-positioned parking space, time off or a long lunch break. There could even be a specific work assignment that has special significance or "perks" attached to it—an industry conference, a special task force or participation in a company-sponsored charitable event, for example.

4. **Acts of service:** This can take many forms, but usually includes involvement of some form on the part of managers and executives in the organization. It could be a breakfast, lunch or dinner served by managers and supervisors. It could also take the form of a meal that is provided or sponsored by company leaders. Even when informally arranged or organized on the spur of the moment, such acts of generosity can have tremendous impact. You may even have experienced something like this yourself—when you've been stuck working late to make an important deadline and the boss ordered (and paid for) pizza delivered to the workplace—a spontaneous and practical show of support and appreciation. Teams don't forget simple gestures like this. Also, consider times when you want to celebrate team success or recognize the whole team's valued contribution to the organization—a catered breakfast or lunch ordered in can go a long way toward expressing genuine appreciation.

There are many variations. One enterprising manager chauffeured a group of rewarded team members to their favorite athletic event where they were free to enjoy food and beverage—knowing that they had their own personal driver who would deliver them safely home after the event. Another team leader rewarded some of his workers by hosting a day of golf at a local golf course, complete with refreshments and gifts of top-quality golf balls. One supervisor recognized her high-performing team members by taking them to a local charity fashion show where they were treated to a celebrity-studded affair, complete with buffet, gift bags and opportunities to win door prizes. The key is the actual participation of the team leader in the expression of recognition or appreciation. That personal presence sends a very strong message of high value—it tells team members that their performance is worth the valuable time and trouble that the team leader is taking to personally express appreciation and affirmation. This is related to the last category.

5. **Time and attention:** Sometimes the most powerful form of recognition is exactly what was just mentioned—the personal presence of the team leader giving time and attention to a valued worker. One of the most common expressions of this is probably "lunch with the boss" at a nice restaurant. For many workers, the real value of such an experience is not the lunch itself, but rather the opportunity to spend time with the team leader—sharing ideas and hearing about future vision and strategic plans. It's a form of *personal access* that workers associate with significance or importance on the team. Sometimes, it can take the form of accompanying the boss on a business trip of some kind—visiting a company site, touring a client's facility or perhaps meeting with an important vendor. The worker is exposed to a bigger picture of the company and becomes privy to the boss's thoughts and conversation. In return, the worker has an opportunity to share their own ideas and input, receiving valuable exposure to and visibility with an important "gatekeeper" to their success in the organization.

UP CLOSE AND PERSONAL

I was brought into an organization to "turn around" a department and bring measurable success in a very short period of time. Part of the challenge I faced was to win over the key players who obviously were put on the defensive by the introduction of an outsider (myself) commissioned to bring about badly needed change. I was given the freedom to hire my chief assistant, but I was also told, "We would like you to interview Gloria. She's been with us for over 15 years, but her department is being phased out. If you don't hire her, we'll have to let her go. But don't feel that you need to let that fact influence your choice." As if I didn't already face a major challenge to win the hearts of the die-hards in the organization!

As it happened, Gloria exhibited a very positive attitude and an enthusiastic energy to do the kind of work I needed—a mix of strong administrative/clerical support and real "people-helping" service. She really blossomed as a member of my team! When she finished one of her first big assignments for me—a printed report—she dropped it on my desk at the close of the day while I was on the phone, intending for me to review it and put it back on her desk with any proposed changes or amendments. When I looked it over, it was great! I put it on her desk with a sticky note attached that just said, "You ROCK!" in big letters (she and I are both music-loving baby-boomers). She posted that little note on the wall of her cubicle, and it stayed there until the day she left the organization.

✓ ACTION STEP

Set up a "Reward Fund" for each team member. Keep a list, spreadsheet or database that identifies the individual things that are important to each member of your team. For one it may be golf or fishing. For another, time off. Others may need public recognition.

Then, put down ideas of how you can match a performance reward with their interest. Keep it updated and current. When the opportunity comes along to reward someone for exceptional performance, you'll have an on-target set of possibilities already lined up.

Team member:	Reward:
1.	
2.	
3.	
4.	
5.	
6.	
7.	
8.	
9.	
10.	

CHAPTER 12:

Building a team culture that weathers the storms and retains your best people

Organizations face tremendous challenges in the next decade. To begin with, a shrinking workforce will make it increasingly difficult *to find and keep* good workers. Companies will face fierce competition for good workers and quality employees. Some corporations already are adopting much more aggressive recruitment strategies in order to find these people and recruit them on college campuses before they enter the marketplace of workers nationwide.

To make matters worse, more and more organizations are experiencing the pain and crisis of mergers and acquisitions—company-wide initiatives that introduce tremendous stress and challenge into the workplace. Add to that the tremendous shifts in industry that are outsourcing current jobs to other international markets and creating whole new jobs in the domestic marketplace. This latest phenomenon is forcing workers to retrain or find whole new roles and skills in order to stay marketable and stay employed. The impact on the workforce in individual organizations can be disastrous—experienced managers know: During a crisis, they are much more likely to lose their *best* people, not their worst! What will you do to prevent losing good people in bad times?

But is this a challenge only during bad times? Research shows that managers face daunting statistics even in good times. A study done less than a decade ago revealed some disturbing realities about the modern workforce. The survey of 2,000 workers revealed:

- **33% are "high risk"**—that is, they are not committed to their current employer and are not planning on sticking around for the next two years
- **39% are "trapped"**—they aren't committed to the organization, but they are planning on staying for the next two years
- **24% are "truly loyal"**—committed to the organization and planning on staying there for at least another two years

The good news is that individual managers have more control over employee retention than ever before. Surveys in the workplace show that workers leave or stay in their positions primarily because of the relationship they have with their boss. It's true. People don't leave organizations as much as they leave managers. Studies show that over 60% of workers who resign their position do so because of a bad boss or manager. The "bad boss syndrome" is the most important reason why employees leave a company. If you learn to manage people well, you'll find it much easier to attract and keep good workers. And research into employee retention has revealed some practical things you can do to develop a "resignation-resistant" team culture, even during times of organizational crisis and change.

To begin with, start implementing the ideas presented in previous chapters! As you develop the ability to inspire your people, you'll also acquire the tools that enable you to build magnetic relationships with them—relationships that attract (and retain) them through influence and respect—instead of forcing relationships through autocratic authority and coercion. These ideas will also help you create a positive work environment that is healthy and attractive to quality workers. Use these additional practical suggestions to gain an even stronger hold on your best people:

Talk a lot—and listen even more

If we haven't already made our point, we'll say it one more time—people have very individualistic wants and needs. The best way to discover what a particular worker needs is to ask. Stay in touch with your team members. Find out how they are doing and how they are feeling about their work, the workplace, the team and the organization. Create an open channel for candid communication. Tell them, "You are important to me and to this team. I want to keep you around, so I want to know what I can do to keep you happy and engaged here." Listen to their ideas and suggestions. Find out what their particular retention "hook" is—for some it will be career path; for others, longevity; for still others, it might be flexibility. Do what you can to address each person's needs with a practical response. Consider the various elements already discussed in previous chapters: Opportunities for learning and growth, meaningful work, challenging assignments, autonomy and freedom in their work. All of these have an important bearing on employee satisfaction.

Stay open

Be willing to consider your workers' ideas and input—especially about how to improve things at work. Be willing to change what you can. Be willing to become their advocate with higher-ups, if it means changing deeply-entrenched policies or procedures.

Stay flexible

More workers are looking for flexibility in their work schedules. The need varies, but your ability to adjust may be the one thing that enables a good worker to stay instead of leave. You may have to lobby hard with HR or higher-ups to get the authority you need to make these concessions, so be prepared to plead your case!

Stay teachable

Get feedback on your own leadership and management! If you are not being a good boss, that may be difficult—your team members probably will be reluctant to give you the honesty and candor you need. In that case, enlist the services of a trusted colleague or HR representative. Bring them into your team. Tell team members, "I want your help to become a better leader and manager. I've asked this person to interview you and get the feedback I need to improve. I want you to be honest with them, knowing that the information you give will remain anonymous." Then follow through—listen openly to the feedback and start making adjustments immediately. The good news is that most of us in the workplace have a short memory when it comes to personal change—we readily accept new attitudes and behavior from fellow workers, and we find it relatively easy to change our attitudes about others when we see them displaying new behavior and new attitudes themselves.

✓ ACTION STEP

List your team members. Identify the retention "hooks" that are most important to each one. Schedule time with each of your team members in the next month to talk about the concepts presented in this chapter. For your own leadership growth, consider a leadership/management "checkup" facilitated by a trusted colleague.

Team member:	Retention "hook":
1.	
2.	
3.	
4.	
5.	
6.	
7.	
8.	
9.	
10.	
11.	
12.	

PART III:

Lead—Achieving World-class Performance

Here's a simple but profound definition of leadership: Leaders are people who are going somewhere ... and taking others with them.

Leadership is about getting somewhere. The "somewhere" that we're talking about is the vision of a leader—it's the final product of their efforts, the destination, the preferred future they are crafting. In fact, here is a simple two-word definition for vision: *Preferred future*. Leaders are driven by their vision for a new, different and better future. They see what doesn't exist ... yet ... and are compelled to make that dream a reality.

Ultimately, the performance of every leader is judged by how well they have achieved their vision for a preferred future. The same is true for you. Your leadership will be measured by how well you have achieved your vision for a better future—a more effective organization, a greater level of service or a higher grade of quality. In this section, we will explore the real benchmark of team leadership—performance—and show you how to assemble the individual members of your team into a cohesive, collaborative and innovative unit that can achieve impact and effectiveness far beyond what they could ever achieve as a group of individuals, laboring separately and independently. Each chapter will give you a practical building block in the all-important process of molding your team into superstar performers in the workplace. And you'll also get the help you need to maintain that high performance, even in the face of bad worker behavior and difficult circumstances.

CHAPTER 13:

Calculating your contribution to the critical path

Vision is central to your role in leading your team to effective performance. It's connected to everything you do as a leader and as an effective manager. And your most effective visionary tool is a compelling team vision statement. This is precisely why we emphasized its importance in Part One. Now you must take your team vision to the next level and connect it with tangible contributions to the success of the organization. So, what is the chief interest of your organization? How does it define success? How does it measure effectiveness? Start by identifying this central concern. It might be customer service, market share, quality manufacturing, health and safety, consumer confidence, timely response, industry recognition or even simple profitability.

Now determine how your team can contribute to this organizational vision. Identify practical things that your team can do to support the successful achievement of your organization's chief interest—look for tangible and measurable contributions. These practical things might include:

- How to improve customer service
- Strategies for keeping current customers and attracting new ones
- Improvements to manufacturing processes that save time or money, increase productivity or create higher quality
- Modifications to processes or products that make for greater safety and public health
- Additions or changes to service that create stronger consumer confidence—ways to improve response time
- Accomplishments that will earn industry recognition and awards
- Savings that will help reduce overhead and contribute to greater profitability

By doing this, you are positioning your team as a group that adds tangible and measurable value to the organization. This will have personal value for *you* when the time comes for your own recognition and reward. You are also helping your team members connect their work with the bigger picture of the organization and its success. This is central to innovation and creativity—the more team members understand their role of support, the better able they will be to provide you with valuable input and ideas for making their contribution better, easier, faster, cheaper and safer.

"Contribution to the critical path" will also give your team members a compelling reason for their hard work and personal engagement—it's a motivational element that connects the team's work with real, tangible purpose and value. It also gives you leverage when addressing difficult situations and individual performance issues.

The key is to develop your critical path contributions with enough detail to provide your team with measurable goals. You can do this with a simple five-step planning process:

Step 1: Identify an organizational value or vision element. Use the vision statement of your organization. Find one aspect of it that will provide a specific focus for this exercise. It might be a value ("excellence") or an outcome ("profitability"). The key is to focus on just one thing at a time.

Step 2: Identify ways you and your team can help the organization realize the value or accomplish the outcome you have selected. For example, if you selected "profitability" to focus on, you might list things like: (1) help grow our sales, (2) cut our expenses or (3) reduce work/increase productivity.

Step 3: Describe specific things you and your team can do to accomplish each of the "ways" you listed in Step 2. The second example—"cut our expenses"—might be supported with specific things like (a) review change orders for charges we may have missed, (b) analyze our budget for potential cuts and savings or (c) research different suppliers who may be able to save us money.

Step 4: Identify individuals or teams in the organization that you need to network with in order to accomplish the things you described in Step 3.
For example, if you wanted to review change orders, you would list the individuals or teams you would need to work with in order to do that—"Robert in the accounting department" or "the accounting team in the main office."

Step 5: Summarize your potential contributions by writing down specific goals for each contribution. Estimate the tangible and measurable value you are trying to achieve through your efforts with each contribution. In the example we're using, it could be as simple as "recover $100,000 in expenses this year." Even if you are unable to achieve the *exact* numbers in your goal, you'll at least have a specific target and a way of measuring *whatever* progress you are able to make toward that goal. This is also the kind of practical information that will give you influence with your boss during your performance review when you have those crucial conversations about raises and promotions.

This exercise will yield a series of specific goals and plans for your team—strategies that will help them add measurable value to the organization. It's well worth your time and effort to sit down with paper and pencil and put these ideas down in black and white—with specific direction that you can share with your team *and* your boss.

✔ ACTION STEP

Use these steps to create action plans for your team. Depending on their level of skill and experience, you may want to include them in this process—they may appreciate the opportunity to explore and develop their own high-impact goals and strategies.

CHAPTER 14:

Creating a collaborative crew that sizzles with synergy

A cohesive team begins to experience high productivity when its members move beyond a simple focus on individual performance and access the powerful effects of collaboration and synergy. Collaboration occurs when we share ourselves and our resources in such a way that all of us together become more effective. Synergy takes place when we share ourselves and our resources in such a way that each of us individually becomes more effective as a result. Here's the key: Collaboration and synergy cannot happen without a clear and coherent team vision. The team vision provides a common focus that channels each team member's knowledge, skills, strengths and ideas into common goals and priorities. In fact, the word "common" is a good descriptor for the dynamic that exists in a cohesive team. True collaboration occurs when these essential elements of a team's experience are held in common: Common vision and values, common goals, common commitment, common information, common communication and common coordination. What does this look like in day-to-day teamwork?

Common vision and values

Common vision and values provide the framework for team collaboration. When teams hold these in common, team members are all headed in the same direction with the same parameters to guide their behavior and effort. For example, when a health services organization holds the vision of "superior service to patients" with the value of "safety," every team in the organization has specific guideposts to define their teamwork. So when the pharmacy team defines their team vision, it reflects the organization's vision and values and comes into alignment with those powerful guidelines: "To provide superior pharmaceutical support to patients and staff with the highest standards of safety and accuracy." Now every member of the pharmacy team has the same guidelines for their work. Every member of the pharmacy team is consistently measuring their efforts with the same simple question: Do my actions represent superior support without sacrificing safety and accuracy? This also enables team members to function together as a team—as a single unit—because they are all guided alike. Thus, the team as a whole is able to raise the same question about its team efforts: Does our action together as a team represent superior support without sacrificing safety and accuracy? When the team can begin to think and act together like this, individual members are better able to understand how and why their individual efforts can contribute to the team's success. This is the foundation for true collaboration—when individual members are more focused on the team's success than their own individual success. Another way of saying this is: True collaboration takes place when each team member accepts that their true measure of individual success is how effectively they contribute to the success of the team as a whole.

Common goals and priorities

True collaboration takes place when a team is working together toward a common goal. Remember, the ultimate success of a team is measured by its performance—how effectively it accomplishes its goals. The goal of a team provides a specific focus for each team member's resources of knowledge, skills, strengths, ideas, time and energy. Collaboration occurs when team members pool their individual resources in order to achieve the team goal.

For example, collaboration for you means that the true value of your individual ability to organize isn't realized until you apply this skill to benefit the team goal (or project). In other words, to function effectively and collaboratively as a member of a team, you must be willing to put more value on your contribution to the team's success than you put on your own individual success. Your individual performance (and success) in the workplace will be judged primarily on how well you contribute to the success of your team.

Common commitment

Without a common commitment to the team and its goals, there never will be true collaboration. Unfortunately, this may be one of the most difficult elements of collaborative teamwork to lead and manage. Our culture has strong elements of individualism (and narcissism!). Younger workers entering the workforce may have a difficult time embracing team success as a higher priority than their own individual success—they may find the status of "star performer" much more appealing than the identity of "team player." Team leaders in the future will have to help team members make the team-success connection and understand that their individual performance will be measured by their contribution to the team effort. This is the new reality in today's workplace—team performance is the priority.

Common information

Collaborative effort on a team requires the constant and consistent sharing of information. The more information that team members have, the more effectively they can serve the success of the team. Keep team members in the dark, and everyone suffers! As a team leader, you'll have to make information sharing a high priority—one of your top agenda items at team meetings. Keep your team members up to date on their performance, on workload issues, on the progress of team projects, on customer and client demands, on the concerns and priorities of higher-ups and on the organization as a whole. But make sure you manage the information flow so that it includes only those items that are of greatest value and priority. Don't just blindly "cc" team members and overload their e-mail boxes—that has the opposite effect—cheapening communication and reducing the value of information in general.

Common communication

All the various forms of communication create the information highway that connects all of your team members. Make sure that you and your team embrace the same *values* for this all-important connection!

- **Open communication** means that all team members are encouraged to share information freely with you and with one another. The more open the communication culture, the less you'll have to deal with gossip and rumors. It will help if you let your team members know that you are an avid and active *listener* and that you value their input and their ideas.
- **Honest communication** implies that you and your team members are reality-based. Send the strong message to your team that you want to know the *truth* of every situation, problem, measurement, effect and outcome.

- **Direct communication** means that you and your team members interact with one another directly without resorting to middlemen in the process. This eliminates the distortion that is so common otherwise—especially from the grapevine and the rumor mill.
- **Interactive communication** defines the information highway as being a two-way street, with traffic going in *both* directions. Be sure that your team members understand you expect them to talk with one another and freely share their ideas, information, opinions and points of view. Above all, make certain that you model these values in your team meetings!

Common coordination and leadership

Collaborative teams aren't headless machines that function automatically and instinctively—they require skilled and effective leadership. Your role as a team leader is to oversee, guide, direct, assess and adjust the various team functions so that the team stays focused and remains productive. A well-led team meeting is one of your most practical and effective tools in this regard. Your meeting agenda should reflect the same functions of collaborative teamwork—resonating with your team vision and values; measuring progress toward the team goal and the completion of team projects; reinforcing common commitment to all of these; and serving as a forum for honest, open, interactive and direct communication.

True collaboration also requires functional work assignments that pool the team's individual resources for the greatest impact and effect. That requires discernment on the part of the team leader—to identify individual skills, knowledge, strengths, gifts and ideas, and to *mobilize* those resources and apply them strategically. That means our pharmacy team (from our previous example) draws on the organizational strength that team member Jeff has when it's time to devise a better way to organize our supplies or our work schedules. So the team leader encourages Jeff to share his ideas with the team, and the team leader encourages the team to consider Jeff's ideas to address the team's needs for organization. And when the team needs to focus on patient or staff interactions, we look to team member Diane to share her ideas and input because of her strength in interpersonal relationships. So the team leader encourages Diane to share her perspective and help other team members to become more effective in this area. In this way, the team leader orchestrates the contributions of individual team members, so each person's resources have the maximum impact and effect, and the team benefits as a whole. This is collaboration at its best and its most valuable!

The magic of synergy

Synergy is a unique byproduct of team collaboration. It occurs when each individual on the team is able to draw on the knowledge, skills, strengths and ideas of other team members in order to become more effective in their individual work assignments. It requires universal access, availability and generosity.

Universal access means each member of the team is able to receive what they need from the other members. Universal availability means that each member of the team makes their individual resources available to the other team members. This ideal requires universal generosity, which means that all the team members embrace the value of sharing their resources.

In our example of the pharmacy team, it means that Tina is able to draw on Jeff's organizational strength to help with her need to become better organized about her work schedule, her workplace, her files or her management of deadlines and workload. It requires that Jeff is willing to take time to share his resources with Tina and coach her to be more effectively and efficiently organized. It means that Roger is able to draw on Diane's relational skills to help him work more effectively with colleagues and clients. And it requires that Diane is willing to make herself available to advise, counsel and coach Roger and other team members. Synergy flows from a common spirit of team camaraderie and generosity, and it's not unusual to find this kind of spirit in cohesive teams that bond together to pursue their vision with passion and determination. It's one of the powerful and exhilarating byproducts of great teamwork. Is such an ideal possible? Like many other elements of effective team dynamics, it's best modeled by a team leader who demonstrates the same kind of availability to come alongside team members and provide various aspects of hands-on support: Time, attention, helpful advice, coaching and resourcing.

✓ ACTION STEP

List your team members and describe each member's set of knowledge, skills, strengths, background, training and special areas of expertise.

Team member:

Member attributes

Knowledge:

Skills:

Strengths:

Background:

Training:

Areas of expertise:

During your team meetings, emphasize the values of collaboration and synergy and show your team members how everyone can benefit from a common passion for effectiveness and a universal spirit of generosity.

Make work assignments that fit each team member's unique set of personal resources.

Suggest ways that team members can help one another in their various areas of responsibility and team activity.

Look for opportunities to share your own personal resources with other team members, through coaching and idea-sharing.

CHAPTER 15:

Cultivating a culture of creativity and accountability

Managers everywhere struggle with the challenge of encouraging high performance among their teams and workers. For many leaders, it's an uphill battle of discouraging and overwhelming proportion. Is there any light at the end of this seemingly unending tunnel of frustrating underperformance and growing worker disengagement? Consider this …

In the 1970s, automobile manufacturers faced a growing competitive threat from Japanese companies that threatened their success and their very future. They adopted a political response by joining with large interest groups and lobbying Congress to apply a crippling tariff to foreign car imports, especially those from Japanese manufacturers. Toyota responded with a creative alternative to importation: In 1984, they sought a joint venture with General Motors to build Toyota products on U.S. soil for sale to the American public, using unionized UAW labor. This new alliance was dubbed New United Motors Manufacturing, Incorporated or NUMMI (pronounced *New Me!*). The first venture in this new alliance took place in a manufacturing plant in Fremont, California that General Motors had closed the year before because of high cost, low quality and a "poor labor climate." The plant was reopened under Toyota leadership, employing the same labor force that General Motors had previously found so "unmanageable." Within a year, it became a low-cost, high-quality production facility, even though it was the least-automated automobile factory in the U.S., and offered union workers the highest wage level in the country.

Toyota applied key manufacturing innovations at the plant, which contributed greatly to its success, but the most significant impact has arguably been the changes they introduced in the way they treated their workers. Toyota created a vastly different management culture that led to high productivity, strong worker engagement, personal accountability and prolific creativity and innovation among its workforce. You can do the same. You can learn from Toyota's management wisdom and generate the same success with your team. Follow the steps in this chapter and learn how to turbocharge your team's productivity and performance by creating a positive and supportive team culture.

What's your style?

It will help you first to understand some practical aspects of creativity, itself. Researchers who have studied creativity in the workplace have identified key styles of innovation—distinct ways that individuals and teams experience and apply creativity at work. Most companies and teams are not in a position to experience all of these styles, but the vast majority are well-positioned to experience two: Goal-based innovation and incremental innovation. Goal-based innovation starts with an outcome. Creativity is expressed and applied as individuals devise creative ways to attain a certain outcome or goal. One of the simplest ways for a worker to express this style of innovation is by having an enlightened manager give them the freedom to do so—by having the boss assign a project or task with a clear outcome and then allow the worker the freedom to devise their own best way of attaining it. This simple act alone—investing the worker with authority and control over their own actions—is often enough to encourage their personal creativity and generate a high level of engagement. It's a basic but powerful way to produce individual accountability through trust and empowerment. It's also a catalyst for developing whole new processes and procedures—new ways to do things easier, better, faster, cheaper and safer.

The power of *kaizen*

The second style of creativity is known as incremental innovation. Toyota has embraced this style of innovation as a key to their success in manufacturing. They have dubbed it *kaizen*—or "continuous improvement." With this style of innovation, the primary focus is on the process instead of the outcome. In a sense, you are dealing with the status quo but looking for ways to tweak existing processes—to make them easier, better, faster, cheaper, safer. With this style of innovation, your team members are your greatest source of ideas—they are closest to the work and are in the best position to discover ways to improve what they are doing. They are the first key to successful *kaizen*—they are the primary source of ideas that fuel this powerful engine of creativity. But they need your help in order to succeed—your role as a leader is the second ingredient for successful creativity!

Follow these nine steps to experience the power of kaizen in your team:

Step 1: Give your people information. The more information your people have, the more creative they can be. Help them understand the "big picture" of the organization and the team's role in the success of the organization—how the team contributes to the critical paths that support the achievement of the company's vision. Show them how their work is connected to the work of other departments and divisions within the organization. Explain the regulations that define the processes and products they use or produce. Teach them the tough realities of costs and expenses—for services, raw materials, supplies, equipment and overhead. Give them the wide-screen view of the business as well—the industry, the marketplace, the competition and the potential clients. The more they know, the better they can think!

Step 2: Connect everything to the vision. Make sure your team keeps a strong focus on its vision—this focus is central to *everything that you do as a team*. The role of creativity is no different. We're not talking about innovation just for the sake of innovation—we're talking about creativity that will help the team to achieve its *vision*—easier, better, faster, cheaper, safer.

Step 3: Ask for their input and their ideas. Let your team know that you want to hear from them. Tell them that you are interested in their input and their ideas. Underscore the valuable place they hold in the structure of the organization—how they are in an ideal position to see things that you don't see and learn things that you need to know about how to do things easier, better, faster, cheaper, safer.

Step 4: Be a good listener. Take time to listen carefully and actively to their ideas. Be available to guide and coach their creativity. Help them to analyze their ideas and refine them to fit the many realities in the workplace. Keep them focused on the vision—help them connect their innovations to the things that really support the performance and success of the team.

Step 5: Support their ideas with experimentation and reward. Be willing to put wheels on their ideas! One of the best ways to judge the practicality of an idea is to simply put it to the test. You don't have to do this whole-handedly, by suddenly instituting a new process or procedure for the whole team—you can do this by sponsoring small experiments that allow one of your team members to try out a new idea and learn from the experience. An experimental approach like this will allow you to tweak new ideas and refine them while minimizing the risk of failure. In any case, always reward new ideas with recognition, even if you feel they are unworkable at the time. Explain to your team member why their idea doesn't fit your present circumstances, but be sure to affirm their willingness to consider new things and bring their thoughts to you.

Step 6: Guide and coach their learning process. Help your team members develop better skill in conceptual thinking and practical application. Help them deconstruct their ideas and evaluate their creative impulses with discernment. As they grow in their ability to observe carefully and think clearly, they will become more creative. Help them to evaluate their experiments with thorough analysis and careful reflection. Ask the right questions in order to guide their thinking:

- Did this help you accomplish your goal easier, better, faster, cheaper and safer? If so, how?
- Is this innovation in alignment with our vision and values?
- Do you see any potential problems with this idea?
- Do you anticipate any obstacles to using this idea?
- What resources will we need in order to adopt this new idea?
- How will this affect other processes, procedures *or people?*

Step 7: Stay flexible. Innovation is all about *change.* If you are going to champion change, you must be willing to flex and adapt—to new processes, procedures, approaches and even assumptions. You must become a constant learner—always willing to gather new information and accommodate appropriate changes in your behavior and mindset. Younger workers on your team will not have problems with flexibility—they have grown up in a world of constant change and variation. But if you are going to lead them and command their respect, you'll have to demonstrate your ability to flex, adapt and change.

Step 8: Take calculated risks. There is no such thing as progress without risk. There is no such thing as experimentation without risk. There is no such thing as learning without risk. There is no such thing as life without risk. There is certainly no such thing as leadership without risk! Start right now by embracing this reality—you'll have to get used to living with risk in your role as a leader and manager. Even so, there is a distinct difference between risk and calculated risk. I live a mile from the Torrey Pines cliffs that line the beach just north of La Jolla, California. The coastal winds that flow eastward over the waves strike the base of the cliffs and are driven straight upward. This natural setting has created one of the most popular locations in the San Diego area for glider flying and hang-gliding. Here's how I define risk: Jumping off the Torrey Pines cliffs. I don't recommend it. It's a long way down with nothing but hard sand and rocks at the bottom. You're going to get hurt—bad. Here's how I define calculated risk: Jumping off the Torrey Pines cliffs attached to a hang-glider. You are less likely to be hurt, but there is still a definite risk involved, albeit a much smaller one. Here is my point: Your role as a leader is not to avoid risk entirely, but to avoid unnecessary risk and to take only those risks that you have carefully calculated. So, before you take a risk on a new idea or innovation—calculate the risk. Ask yourself: What could possibly go wrong? What is the worst thing that could happen? These questions will introduce careful reflection and give you a much better way to determine if the potential benefit of the new idea outweighs the potential risk of failure.

Step 9: Don't punish mistakes. Mistakes in life are like risks—they are unavoidable. It's only a matter of time before you or one of your team members will make one. Your choice is not whether you'll make them, but how you'll respond to them. Decide now that you'll handle mistakes as positively and constructively as you can. Certainly, address them—don't sweep them under the rug of denial. By all means, focus on correction rather than punishment—when your team members make a mistake, they need your support and your help to fix the situation, not fix the blame. Always use mistakes as learning opportunities, and teach your people to do the same. One leader has said, if we're not making any mistakes, we're not trying hard enough to succeed! Let that be your motto as a leader and as a team. So make mistakes count. Use mistakes to help you learn, grow, adapt and succeed the next time. Model this clear-headed approach to your team. Here is some encouragement for you in this process: If you do a good job of calculating risks, the chances are good that your mistakes will be much less catastrophic and much more bearable as a result.

If you follow these nine simple steps, you'll create a team culture that encourages and supports creativity and innovation. You'll begin to experience the power of *kaizen*—continuous improvement—and you'll engage the energy and enthusiasm of your team. You'll also do something else—you'll cultivate a strong sense of personal accountability among your team members. This will enable you and your team to bring this new experience of creativity into the arena of evaluation, which is one of the most important functions of a high-performing team.

Change your team culture

Evaluation is traditionally associated with the role of management. But in high-performing teams, individual workers develop such a strong degree of accountability that they begin to participate meaningfully in self-assessment and personal evaluation. There is a good illustration of this in the Toyota manufacturing process. In Toyota plants, workers on the production line are given the authority to actually stop the production line and bring production to a halt if they see any problems that they feel need to be addressed. Toyota has even given an added twist to this policy—stops to the production line are signaled by music instead of by alarms. And each team on the production line chooses their "theme music" so that when the process is halted, the location of the stop is immediately identified by the distinctive music that is played throughout the factory. This twist might be considered a small thing, but it's another way that Toyota underscores the value of accountability and authority. Team members know that they have control over the production process, and they also have accountability for that control. You can help your team members develop greater personal accountability by making simple but profound changes in your team culture.

Become an ally instead of an adversary

Traditional approaches to management make the team leader the "bad guy" in the evaluation process, invested with the responsibility to debrief the work and discover any ways that the work could have been done better (or easier, faster, cheaper, safer). Change this by inviting team members to participate in the evaluation process. Put as much of this responsibility in their hands as you can. Position the process as one that focuses more on creativity rather than correction. Tell them that you are interested in their ideas for continuous improvement. Explain to them that they are in the best position to see ways to do their work easier, better, faster, cheaper, safer.

Connect evaluation with vision and outcomes

Make sure your team members keep the team vision at the center of the evaluation process. The more you help them make this connection, the better they will understand the vision and its importance to high performance. Here's another great byproduct of this emphasis: Your team members will also be more likely to *internalize* the vision and really take ownership of it. And when you connect the evaluation process with *outcomes*, you are keeping evaluation on track where it will have the most practical application and value.

Support evaluation with your time and attention

Set aside time during your team meetings to debrief projects and work assignments and harvest your team members' ideas for improvement and innovation. If you don't support the evaluation process with your time and attention, your team members will not believe that you really believe in its importance. One aspect of this is your own availability to listen to your team's feedback and ideas and guide and coach their process of evaluation. Another important ingredient is your willingness to evaluate *your own work* and even invite feedback from team members about it!

Evaluate everything

Model the practice of continuous and consistent evaluation. Call it "debriefing" if you like (it may be a more positive term to use) but keep the practice in front of your team members all the time. Evaluate big projects; evaluate small work assignments. Evaluate old processes; evaluate new plans. Evaluate all outcomes. Keep asking the same question: *Is there any way to do this easier, better, faster, cheaper, safer?* Stay open to their ideas and feedback.

Respond appropriately—with affirmation and praise

When you have finished with the evaluation process, remember to respond appropriately with affirmation and praise. This is the positive side of feedback, but it's too often eclipsed by the *negative* side (criticism and correction). When you involve your team members in the evaluation process, constructive criticism is a natural byproduct—they will surface many ideas about how the work could have been done easier, better, faster, cheaper, safer. Just be sure that team members also hear affirmation and praise from *you* about the *positive* aspects of their work.

Reinforce evaluation with recognition and reward

Always affirm your team members when they offer their evaluations. Recognize their good ideas, but also recognize them for participating in the evaluation process itself. Reward their efforts, even if you do so with just a simple statement of recognition and affirmation. Remember what Ken Blanchard reminds us: *What gets recognized gets repeated.*

✓ ACTION STEP

Start talking with your team members *now* about evaluation and continuous improvement. Explain the purpose and focus of evaluation (how to support the vision in ways that are easier, better, faster, cheaper, safer). Set aside time in your next team meeting to debrief any key projects or assignments.

CHAPTER 16:

Conquering crisis, conflict, conduct and contingency

Performance is never more important than when conditions are less than ideal—your real test of leadership happens when the heat is on, and you are faced with difficult situations or challenging behavior. How you respond during tough times will be one of the most important indicators of your true capacity to lead well and manage effectively. In each section of this chapter, you'll gain fresh insight into the four major challenges you'll face as a leader, and you'll receive practical tools and strategies that will enable you to keep your team on track with continued high performance, even when the going gets tough.

Dealing with the "problem child"

It's only a matter of time before you'll have to deal with a team member's poor behavior or inadequate performance. Determine at the outset that you'll adopt the right mindset. Don't ever take a team member's misbehavior personally. If you view their behavior as a personal affront to your authority, you are in danger of getting emotionally hooked into an attitude that will quickly lead you to anger and inappropriate response. Keep a healthy emotional distance. Remind yourself that your role as a manager is to help each of your team members to perform at the highest level of effectiveness. Keep this purpose at the forefront of your thinking as you use the following 10 steps to help you do just that:

1. **Clarify the problem.** Make sure your team member knows that there is a problem and understands the exact nature of the problem. Use this phrase to begin your conversation: *Were you aware ... ?* It will introduce the topic of your discussion, give your team member the benefit of the doubt and invite their response. You'll be surprised how often a team member will respond to this question with a simple "No, I wasn't aware."

2. **Listen carefully and respectfully.** Your greatest tool of influence is your own positive and healthy behavior. When you listen well, you demonstrate respect, value, courtesy and maturity. You set the stage for much more positive communication.

3. **Identify their point of view.** Hear them out. Do your best to understand their situations, their reasoning and their point of view. People have reasons for their behavior—look behind your team member's actions and identify their reasons. Make sure team members understand exactly what you expect from them. Look for any confusion with regard to their assignment, outcomes or measurements for success. Identify any performance obstacles that they need help in addressing. Be sure they have all the tools, training or resources they need to be successful. Use this phrase: *Help me understand …* as a way to invite their response. If you need to, take notes to help you listen carefully and accurately.

4. **Emphasize the team vision.** Put the team vision at the center of the conversation—remind your team member of the vision that they have committed to (as every other team member has).

5. **Put accountability in their hands.** Ask your team members to clarify how this behavior supports the team vision. Use the *"help me understand"* phrase to prompt a response. This step reinforces the culture of personal accountability you are creating with your team—especially with regard to evaluation.

6. **Explain the negative impact of the behavior.** Show how the behavior impacts the team, the client or customer and the organization. Show how the behavior impedes progress toward the team vision. Connect the poor behavior to individual emotional triggers and motivations. Help team members understand how they are ultimately hurting themselves by not addressing the problem.

7. **Invite collaboration.** Ask team members for their input. Use this phrase to help prompt a response: *What do you think would be a better approach?*

8. **Offer your support.** Use these phrases to emphasize your willingness to help and to also identify practical ways to do it: *How can I help you succeed? What can I do to help you?*

9. **Agree on an appropriate response.** Underscore this agreement with a symbolic but tangible expression of commitment. For example, you can ask your team member to "give me your word that you'll change this" problem behavior. You can also ask for this commitment in writing—by using a simple e-mail message to that effect.

10. **End with affirmation.** State your confidence that they will address the issue. Remind them of their other positive contributions and their value to the team and its success.

A word of advice. Solve potential performance problems ahead of time by doing a thorough job of hiring. If you hire well, you'll solve a lot of behavior and conduct problems before they happen. In the interviewing process, look for qualities in the candidate that fit your team demands (e.g., reliability, industriousness, patience, honesty). Always keep your team vision in the foreground, and hire people who already show alignment with the central elements of your vision and values. For example, if you are in the health services industry, your team vision is likely to contain a strong emphasis on serving people. When you are hiring team members, look for candidates who already hold this value and demonstrate a keen interest in (and history of) work that expresses it.

Acting as referee

Conflict isn't just a normal part of team life—it's a *necessary* path to greater team effectiveness. Yes, it's true—studies of effective teams show that *every* effective team passes through a phase of development that is marked by conflict and discord. This experience of dissension and disagreement is a natural byproduct of the diversity of any effective team. It happens because team members have different personalities, strengths, points of view, expectations, apprehensions and personal and professional concerns.

Before team members can function effectively (and efficiently) together, they must resolve enough of their differences to embrace one another as trusted, respected and appreciated colleagues. This process of resolution takes time, effort, determination and skill. Your role as a team leader is central to this process. You must become a mediator for your team members—not to artificially "settle" disagreements by autocratic decree, but by helping them interact in a healthy way and develop an appropriate level of acceptance and consensus. Here are the essential steps you need to take to lead your team through conflict and disagreement:

1. **Proceed with caution.** Conflict can be a very incendiary experience! Emotions can run high, and sensitive egos are apt to inflame the process. Proceed slowly, carefully and cautiously. Your behavior will set the tone for the interactions that follow.

2. **Stay calm.** Your team members will take their emotional "cues" from you. If you show anger in the way you look and sound, they will respond in kind—their anger will increase and make any interaction more difficult to pursue with objectivity.

3. **Stay objective.** Your initial goal is to bring clarity to the discussion, not take sides. Do all you can to mentally set aside any bias or prejudice you have about the team members or their issues.

4. **Listen.** Carefully. To everyone. Don't interrupt. Take notes if it helps. Use clarifying questions to be sure you understand what is being said. You have two main goals in this process …

   - *Find the facts.* This is your first goal in the listening process. Identify what is true. Find out what happened—what people said, did, intended, etc. Try to gain as accurate a picture as possible of the circumstances.

   - *Clarify each person's point of view.* Point of view is the way a person understands, interprets, evaluates or values the facts. Point of view can be frustratingly idiosyncratic. One person's evaluation of the facts can be radically different from another's. For example, one team member's failure to meet a deadline for their contribution to a team assignment may feel like a minor failure to them, but another team member may identify it as a serious betrayal of trust. Who is right in this regard? There is no dispute about the fact of the failure itself, but team members may feel very differently about the *essential value* or *significance* of that failure—what it really *means* in the end. *Validation* is a powerful way to express understanding of a person's point of view. Validation doesn't necessarily mean that you *agree* with a team member's point of view— only that you *understand it*. Remember what validation sounds like: *I think if I were in your situation, seeing things (or understanding things) from your point of view, I would probably feel the same way.*

5. **Resolve any misunderstandings in communication.** This may very well be the greatest value that an objective listener can bring to the conflict—a calm and rational collecting of accurate information and opinions.

6. **State your understanding of the situation and each person's point of view.** This alone may actually end the conflict. Human nature explains why—the chief concern of many people in conflict is to simply have their point of view understood and validated. For them, validation is the "principle of the thing"—their main goal in arbitration. When they are convinced that their position has been understood, they are often more than willing to make concessions or even relinquish demands.

7. **Avoid scapegoating or blaming.** The goal of this process is not to identify a villain for the piece—it's to encourage personal accountability and cultivate understanding and mutual commitment to a solution.

8. **Focus on the vision.** Remind team members of the team vision and how their actions in the given situation are connected to it. Show how their behavior impacts the vision—for better or for worse. The team vision needs to dominate and define everything that you do as a team. Your team members need to hear loud and clear that nothing is more important than the team vision. It's more important than their opinions, attitudes, needs and preferences. Everything they think and do as team members must serve the team vision above all else. That doesn't mean that their needs are not important—it only means that the team vision is *more* important. Keep this in mind: *The more you position the team vision in the center of your teamwork, the more effectively you'll resolve team conflict.*

9. **Affirm each team member's value.** Show how and what they contribute to the success of the team. Identify each person's mix of knowledge, talent, skill, training, personality and experience. Show how the positive elements in this mix outweigh the negative. Your goal is to help each team member see the value of every other team member's contribution to the success of the team and to develop a genuine appreciation for their colleagues. You want your team members to be able to look beyond their differences and embrace their contributions: *Yeah, Bob can be a little cantankerous from time to time, but it's only because he really knows his stuff and wants to make sure we all get it right as a team. That's the kind of energy and passion for excellence that we need to succeed.*

10. **Ask for recommendations.** Invite their input and ideas. Remember: People support what they help to create. The more opportunity each person has for sharing ideas and suggestions, the more likely you'll be to gain their support for resolution.

11. **Broker each person's requests.** Be willing to represent each person's requests in a positive way to the other side of the conflict. Help each person to understand the point of view of the other. Point out similarities in each person's position or view. Require each person to show how their request will help the whole team support and achieve the team vision.

12. **Work toward mutual respect, appreciation and support.** These are the ingredients of *trust* on a team. As trust levels rise on a team, so does productivity. This has been revealed by detailed studies of high-performing teams. Here's the challenge: There is no quick and easy way to build trust on a team! The only way to do that is through the long and tough process of addressing and resolving conflict. What may surprise you as a leader is that the *process* is more important than the *product*. In other words, the resolution you achieve is less important than the process that team members use in order to achieve it. It's through the process that team members develop better understanding of each other, and with it, they gain greater respect, greater appreciation, mutual trust and genuine support for one another's successful contributions to the team. These elements are many times more important to your team's long-term success than the resolution of any single problem or situation.

13. **Ask for commitment.** Once you have come to a solution or resolution, don't assume that each person will support it. Ask for a verbal commitment. Make it simple and straightforward: *Bob, will you commit to this solution and support it?*

Managing Murphy

If you want to be a high performing leader, adopt the same mindset toward problems that you have adopted toward risk: Accept the fact that problems are a part of life. They happen. You can't prevent them entirely. Your primary goal should not be to avoid problems, but to anticipate them and address them appropriately when they happen. Your secondary goal should be to focus only on those problems that you really need to address. The first goal is fairly simple to achieve—just analyze every situation with Murphy's Law firmly in hand. Murphy's Law provides a simple method for calculating risk and anticipating problems. Murphy's Law reminds us: *Anything that* can *go wrong* will *go wrong.* Applying Murphy's Law is as simple as raising the question "What can possibly go wrong?" and furnishing appropriate responses. Anticipating problems is the most valuable (and practical) step toward *solving* them. Do the right critical thinking at the outset, and you'll be miles ahead in the application phase and have fewer obstacles to your and your team's high performance.

You must also be willing to face the reality that *you* may be your own biggest obstacle to high performance. This can easily happen if you accept too many problems as your own and spend your valuable time addressing problems that other people could (and should) solve. To avoid this, you must equip and empower your team members to become effective problem solvers. Most managers will find this difficult because the vast majority of managers and supervisors are intuitive problem solvers—they have no explicit or well-defined method apart from their own common sense and natural analytical gifts. You can easily overcome this barrier by familiarizing yourself with this simple but effective problem-solving method:

Step 1: Define the key issue at the center of the problem. This is more difficult than it appears. Many issues may be potentially relevant, but you must identify which one is central to the problem (and thus, the solution!).

Step 2: Write down a statement of the problem. This is a simple but powerful exercise that will help clarify your thinking. It will also give you a brief definition of the problem, which will enable you to communicate the problem clearly to colleagues and team members and engage them in helping to generate solutions.

Step 3: Determine the most relevant factors. Think of anything that has a direct bearing on the situation.

Step 4: Develop alternative solutions. Generate as many as you can. Don't evaluate any solutions *yet*—keep that step in the process separate from this one. Be as creative as you can. Think as unconventionally as possible. It doesn't matter how wild or crazy your ideas are—at this stage of the process, there is simply no risk of failure (since your ideas are just on paper at this point).

Step 5: List the advantages and disadvantages of each. I recommend you use a two-column approach—it's a remarkably *visible* way of making comparisons. If you generate a good solution, there is a good chance you'll *see it* right away when you start compiling your columns. This simple exercise may also be of value to you when it comes time to choose a solution and actually pursue it. If the solution has an overwhelming majority of advantages, it will be visibly apparent. This may give you more confidence to choose the solution and accept the risk to make it viable and workable.

Step 6: Summarize the merits of each alternative. Drill down to a big-picture summary of the strengths of each solution.

Step 7: Choose the alternative that best fits your situation. By this phase of the exercise, you'll have a much better grasp of your situation *and* your solutions— you'll have done the thorough, thoughtful work that leads to greater insight and better understanding.

Conquering crisis

Crisis is becoming a much more common phenomenon in organizations today. The volatility of the national and global marketplace may be one of the reasons. Or it may be due to the vast and rapid changes that occur in technology and science. In any case, growing numbers of the managers and executives I train tell me that their organizations are experiencing one or more crises of some kind. Increasingly, you'll not have the luxury of avoiding crisis—you'll have to learn how to manage and achieve high performance in the midst of crisis. And—as with so much of what you do—your team vision is central to your ability to cope with crisis and produce effective results in spite of it.

Team vision is the most stabilizing force during crisis because vision doesn't change—even in the midst of crisis. Granted, there are many things that *can* and *do* change during crisis, but vision isn't one of them. Remember, vision is your preferred future. Why would your preference for the future change because of circumstances or problems? It doesn't. Crisis doesn't change your destination as a team (i.e., your vision, where you are headed, it only changes the landscape. The key to high performance during crisis is to keep the vision firmly in front of the team. It will keep your people focused on what really matters—what they can accomplish toward achieving their vision. To keep your team performing at their best during a crisis, follow these simple guidelines:

1. **Set smaller, achievable goals.** Help your team to focus on smaller, more short-term goals. Be sure they are in alignment with the team vision—helping you get where you want to go.

2. **Modify your strategy.** Make whatever adjustments are necessary in order to accommodate the changes in your current situation.

3. **Stay flexible.** Be willing to change the usual ways you do things if it will help your team to be more effective in the midst of your new circumstances. Don't compromise on safety procedures, but don't get stuck in current ways of doing things just because of your unwillingness to accept different approaches or processes.

4. **Give people the stuff they need.** Provide logistical support. Make sure your team members have the tools, training, resources and support they need in order to perform at their most effective. Be prepared to address any organizational or bureaucratic obstacles to their success.

5. **Give people the lift they need.** Provide *emotional* support. Use appropriate words that S.A.V.E. to address their needs for encouragement, confidence, support and optimism.

6. **Recognize, reward and celebrate.** Crisis requires you to become the head cheerleader of your team. Your people will need the encouragement. They will also need the right focus. And they will respond to the models of success you raise as exemplary when you recognize and reward the right kind of performance. So find success wherever you can! Recognize and reward individual effectiveness, and celebrate what your team achieves together.

Managing mergers and succeeding at succession

One of the most challenging scenarios for managers today is managing the changes (and frequent crises) that occur from merger or acquisition. My extensive experience in training executives and managers has convinced me that mergers and acquisitions are the most common sources of organizational change in business today. If you serve in the non-profit or the public sector, don't read this last statement and think that you are immune from organizational change, because the second most common source of organizational change today is leadership succession. When these things happen, you are certain to experience the discomfort (or trauma!) of crisis and change. Your key to survival during these challenging times of transition is to give leadership to successful performance. Here are some keys to help you:

1. **Adopt a supportive stance.** Even when you have reservations about the changes that are coming down from higher management, become a staunch supporter. Higher-ups won't appreciate a rebel in their ranks—they are looking for people who will support the changes and make them successful. If you decide that you would rather leave the new organization than stay and become part of the new culture, it's vital that you continue to support the change until you leave. Your continued positive attitude and effective leadership is essential to support and protect your professional reputation.

2. **Bring your team vision in alignment with the new organizational vision.** The toughest changes to impose are those that signal a new organizational culture. Your formula for team success doesn't change when this happens. Make sure your team vision is in alignment with the new vision that is being installed by executive leadership.

3. **Be a cheerleader *to* your team.** Actively support the changes and communicate thoroughly about them to your team: Explain the changes; show how the changes are meant to help the organization succeed; connect the changes with your team's vision and work; and address your team members' concerns about the changes.

4. **Keep your team focused on the new vision.** Build your team's goals around the new vision for success and high performance. Help each team member to connect their work with the new organizational and team vision. Establish new benchmarks for their work and their high performance.

5. **Support the vision with recognition and reward.** Keep your eyes open for team members who demonstrate support for the new vision through their behavior and performance. Find tangible and meaningful ways to reward them. Recognize them publicly and raise them up as models for the rest of the team.

6. **Be a cheerleader *for* your team.** Showcase your team members' successes to your boss. Give them lots of public credit. Find ways to publicize their good work in the organization as a whole (e.g., mentions in departmental meetings, special announcements, articles in the organizational newsletter).

UP CLOSE AND PERSONAL

A community health services organization in the western U.S. was actually a better organization during crisis than they were during "business as usual." When their facility was rendered unusable because of an "act of God," the staff was forced to completely rethink their normal way of doing things. They exercised the right kind of creativity and were soon dispensing critical services from temporarily vacant store fronts, donated recreational vehicles and open-air locations under tents pitched in vacant lots. The managers and staff weren't whining about conditions—they were galvanized by their common commitment to the vision of the organization! They were passionate about providing lifesaving health services to a segment of the community that badly needed them. And they were energized by their own creative solutions to the contingencies of their current crisis. Their vision made the difference—it kept them focused and high-performing.

✓ACTION STEP 1

The next time you have to address a team member's problem behavior, set aside time to plan and prepare your strategy—how you'll proceed and what you'll say. Write out a script for this important conversation—carefully compose exactly what you want to say and how you want to phrase it. Show your script to a trusted colleague and get feedback from them. Use their suggestions to refine your script. Practice your script until it becomes comfortable and feels less awkward. Then meet with your team member privately and confront their behavior.

Problem behavior:

Applied conversation script:

✓ ACTION STEP 2

The next time you have a problem to solve, use it to create an opportunity to teach problem-solving to your team. How do you do this? Set aside a healthy amount of time during your next team meeting for this very purpose. Put the problem in front of your team. Take them through the steps of the problem-solving method outlined above. Use the team meeting as a setting where they can share their ideas and work together as a group. You can lead the discussion and make sure things stay on track. You can also coach the process by evaluating the team's ideas and input along the way—if they get sidetracked or if their ideas are off-kilter, you can step in and provide appropriate correction and redirection.

You can also use the problem-solving method to guide and coach *individual* team members as they learn how to solve problems. You can work with them one-on-one using a problem that they have brought to you to solve.

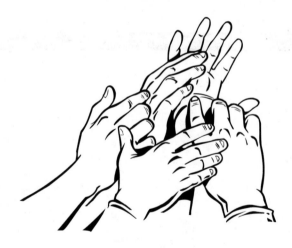

PART IV:

Succeed—Receiving Recognition, Reward, Raises and Rank

This is the selfish section of the book—this is where you make the vital connection between your team's success and your success. Don't think that your success as a team leader will automatically translate to your own personal recognition and reward. Like anything else you do as a leader, you must take initiative and lead this process as well. If you want to enjoy the fruits of your success—raises and promotions—you must be willing to cultivate them by paying close attention to critical aspects of your own performance and professional identity.

In the pages that follow, you'll find a treasure trove of practical tips, pointers and experience-derived advice. Take advantage of these helpful directives—they come from executive coaches, career advisors, industry experts and high-level headhunters.

CHAPTER 17:

Succeeding at your real job

Do you know what your real job description is? I'm not talking about the document you were given during your hiring process. I'm referring to the real measure of your successful performance. More often than not, you won't discover this until after you are hired. Your real job description consists of the critical accomplishments that you were hired to produce—the tangible value that you are expected to bring to your work, your boss and your organization. Let me explain.

If you're interested in a raise or a promotion, you can get the same advice from any management coach or good book. They'll tell you the same thing. If you want to be able to reasonably and persuasively ask your boss for a raise, you'll have to prepare for that request—and you'll have to prepare months in advance. In other words, if you want to request a raise at your next performance review in twelve months, you'll have to start now by focusing on the things you need to accomplish in the next twelve months that will provide your boss with a compelling reason for granting you that raise. So the question is: *What do you have to accomplish in the next twelve months that will enable you to march into your boss's office and persuasively demand a raise?* The answer to that question is the content of your real job description.

In other words, the answer to that question depends greatly on what your boss wants you to accomplish. Do you know what that is? Have you had that conversation with your boss? If you haven't, that is where you need to begin—now. The alternative is to try to read your boss's mind. If you aren't a good mind reader, you'll end up spinning your wheels and spending your energy on the wrong goals and tasks. If you are a leader, you'll be smarter than that. Plan now to have a direct and honest sit-down with your boss. Present your ambitions for success. Explain your commitment to high performance in your role. And ask the all-important question: *Boss, what do I have to accomplish in the next six to twelve months to be able to reasonably expect a raise?* If your ambitions go beyond simple raises to expanded assignments and advancement, then ask that question as well. Get the answer you need to make sure you are on track with your efforts in your current leadership role.

✓ACTION STEP

Schedule time with your boss for the discussion outlined above. Ask the all-important question. Be prepared to listen carefully. Ask your boss directly: *What can I reasonably expect if I succeed?* Then ask your boss for a commitment—to recognize your success appropriately when you have delivered the desired results. Now … *get busy doing the things that will help you achieve that result.*

CHAPTER 18:

Succeeding at your most important job

Now that you're working in the right direction, make sure that you're working in the right way. The right way is to make your boss look good. That is your most important job. (After all, that's why your boss hired you in the first place!) To do this well, you must first adopt the right mindset toward your boss. Having a positive attitude toward your boss is essential—and it may be your biggest challenge. Surveys in the workplace have revealed the importance of the "boss" relationship and its inherent problems—over sixty percent of individuals who resign a position do so because of a bad boss or manager. If you want to succeed in your organization, you must understand that your boss is the gatekeeper of that success. You must value the role your boss plays in your success—in the organization and in your future beyond it. And you must learn to work with and through your boss, not against your boss. If you develop an adversarial relationship with the person you report to, you'll close the gate to your own success and turn your professional future into a dead-end street. Don't make that mistake. Learn how to build a positive relationship with your boss that will propel you to greater heights of success and achievement. The suggestions that follow will enable you to do just that.

1. **Flex.** You must be willing to adapt to your boss and not expect your boss to adapt to you. To begin with, adapt to your boss's *management* style. If your boss takes a direct, hands-on approach, don't be offended. Make sure that you are well-prepared for any questions about what you are doing, how you are progressing on an assignment or what results you are achieving. If you feel you are being micromanaged, then respond with plenty of information and details. Take the initiative to ask for regular meetings where you can keep the boss well-informed and allay any fears about your work. If your boss prefers a more informal, hands-off approach, then be prepared to work more independently and establish your own benchmarks and processes for monitoring work and progress. Identify your boss's style of communication, and adapt to that, too. Your boss may prefer verbal communication—quick, informal, conversational updates in the hallways, over the phone or in a team meeting. Or your boss may prefer details in writing—regular e-mails, lengthy reports, detailed plans

or special memos. Adapt to your boss's organizational preferences as well—filing systems, reporting systems and processes and procedures. Last, be willing to arrange your schedule around your boss's availability—when your boss prefers team meetings, individual appointments, project meetings, etc.

2. **Take initiative.** Don't do just the work your boss asks you to do. Look around. Be proactive. If you see something that needs to be done, do it. If you see a problem that needs to be solved, solve it. Don't wait to be asked. Take ownership of the organization, and take initiative to make it better. The next point is closely allied with this.

3. **Volunteer.** Be willing to step forward and take on assignments—especially the tough ones that nobody else wants. Taking on the tough assignment guarantees success. To begin with, your boss will appreciate your willingness to do it without begin coerced. And you may be able to use the assignment to gain concessions from the boss for more resources (e.g., time, money or even staff). Here's another advantage—even if your performance is less than stellar, no one is likely to complain. (If they do, they may get stuck with the next tough job!) You also should look for work assignments that will stretch you and help you to expand your skill set, experience more visibility and develop greater self-confidence.

4. **Produce.** Earn the reputation of being someone who produces results—someone who will make things happen. I find a lot more "talking" in organizations than I find "doing." You'll create real value for yourself if you become known for your ability to execute plans, accomplish goals and achieve results. By all means, be the kind of person who will do what you say you'll do. This not only demonstrates your value—it also earns you respect.

5. **Function autonomously.** Be the kind of worker who doesn't need constant help, attention or encouragement from the boss. Bosses are busy enough with their own concerns. They don't need to be plagued with constant questions, requests or demands from subordinates. They appreciate team members who can function effectively with a minimal need for their valuable time and attention.

6. **Bring value.** Discover and present ways to increase revenue, savings or productivity. Every organization ultimately exists only as long as they have the finances to do so. Since money is important to every organization, figure out how to help your organization make it, save it or stretch it. When you do that, you are not only bringing real value to your organization, you are able to measure that value in a very tangible way.

   Be prepared to look beyond the obvious—don't think "my team is in a support function … we don't have anything to do with revenue." If your team provides stellar support, they may at some point be responsible for earning a customer's referral for more business. If that happens, your team has just increased the company's revenues. And if you can track the business that the newly referred customer is providing, then you can measure your team's contribution to company revenue in specific, monetary amounts. Similarly, if you've solved a customer's problem and thereby avoided losing them as a customer, you've saved the company measurable costs since most marketing departments know exactly what the organization spends to attract a new customer. And don't say to yourself, "I'm a good leader, but I don't have any way of measuring that in specific, monetary amounts." If your effective team leadership has lowered turnover on your team, then you can certainly measure that impact in specific, monetary amounts since the industry standard for replacing a worker is now roughly two and a half times the worker's annual salary. Do the math, and you'll have a tangible number to share with your boss.

7. **Offer help.** Be willing to help your boss succeed in whatever way you can. Be available to lend your skills, strengths, time and effort to help your boss become more efficient and more effective. When your boss succeeds, so do you.

8. **Provide support.** The most basic way to provide support is simply to do your own job well—especially the work that supports the projects and tasks that are important to your boss. By all means, make sure your work is complete and well-organized. If your boss needs anything explained or interpreted, be sure to do so—don't ever cause your boss to appear unprepared, ignorant or disorganized. Get enrolled in your boss's projects. Whatever your boss considers important, *you* should consider important. If your boss has a pet project, be sure to send the message that *you* are available to help make that project a success. You can also provide support by finding appropriate (and subtle) ways to "market" your boss by letting people in the organization know where the boss has strengths to contribute and how the boss has helped you and your team succeed.

9. **Give cover.** Watch your boss's back—the moment you see a problem brewing, make sure you let the boss know what's going on. You can also help your boss by being a buffer for your team—interpreting the boss's behavior, mollifying a strong management style, softening harsh words and expressing public support for the boss in the face of unfair criticism or misunderstanding. You can also watch out for your boss by anticipating the requests and demands of your boss's boss.

10. **Solve your boss's problems.** Napoleon Bonaparte is famous for telling his generals, "Don't bring me problems. I have enough problems of my own. Bring me *solutions!*" Most bosses have the same mindset—they have enough problems of their own without having subordinates add to their burden. If you ever have to alert the boss to a problem, always propose a solution to address it. The chances are good your boss will accept your solution without much debate.

11. **Take items off your boss's plate.** This is reverse delegation. You know how difficult it is for *you* to delegate—finding the right person, selling them on the idea, getting them to "buy in" and agree to more work. Think of how *any* boss would feel if one of their subordinates *volunteered* to take on some of their more annoying or time-consuming assignments. The key is to free up the boss to spend time and energy on the more important work—the work that creates greater impact and effectiveness in the long run.

12. **Get the boss enrolled in your projects.** This gains you important visibility and helps your boss see firsthand what you are doing and how you are bringing value to the team and your boss's area of responsibility. The most basic way to do this is to show your boss how your team's work is going to make a contribution to the success of the organization. It also helps if you can show how your team's work supports your boss's key interests and pet projects.

   Another simple way you can gain valuable visibility and support is to recruit your boss to help you with team recognition and reward. Ask the boss to write short congratulatory notes to the high performers on your team; ask the boss to hand out award certificates or gifts; have the boss show up at a special reward event you have organized for your team (e.g., breakfast or lunch) and say a few words of congratulations. When this happens, everybody wins. Your team members get a special message of recognition ("Wow, the 'big boss' showed up!"); you look good in front of your boss; and the boss looks good in front of your team. Your team will love any boss that supports you, their favorite leader! Don't underestimate the value of this simple activity—if you want to gain raises and promotions, it's vital that your boss have a positive, impressive, firsthand acquaintance with your work and your impact.

13. **Don't burn any bridges.** When it's time to leave, make sure you do so with the utmost of professionalism. Leave as positively as you can—even if you are leaving because of less than ideal circumstances (*especially* if you are leaving because of less than ideal circumstances!). Don't kick the boss on the way out the door—you may live to regret any negative image of yourself that you leave behind. Professional networks can be a lot smaller and tighter than we think—word about your behavior and reputation may travel faster through that network (and through your industry) than you realize. You always want to leave any organization with as positive a reputation and image as you possibly can.

   If you inherit a bad boss and you know from the outset that it's going to be a difficult relationship, don't start off on the wrong foot. Don't think, "It really doesn't matter how I treat this person—I'm going to leave anyway." The only person you are likely to injure with that mindset is yourself. If you value your career, your professional goals, your reputation, your image and your standing in the industry, you'll serve your boss as positively and as supportively as you possibly can before you finally leave. In fact, you should never resign a position until you have done everything possible to work effectively with your boss and make that all-important relationship viable and workable for both of you.

Only use resignation as your very last resort. It will help you in the long run if you can learn how to work with difficult people—maintaining a constructive relationship with them while keeping a positive attitude. You'll discover the value of that skill as you progress in your career.

UP CLOSE AND PERSONAL

A young and ambitious executive was recruited by the organization's exec to join his team and turn around a department that had fallen on hard times. "You have one year to turn things around and get it back on its feet" the exec told the new hire. "If you don't accomplish your assignment, you'll be terminated." The eager manager accepted the challenge. Within six months, he had made significant headway and told the exec that he and his team were likely to achieve their ambitious goals for growth and development. "I want to know if you hit your numbers," the exec told him. "If you do, I want you to come and get me, no matter where I am or what I'm doing. I want to go to your department and personally congratulate your people."

When the numbers came in and signaled the team's success, the department manager sent a representative to bring "the old man" into the department. The exec left an important meeting to come into the department and offer enthusiastic congratulations and to praise the team (and its leader) for their impressive achievement. The atmosphere was electric! Everyone in the room came away with an incredible feeling of success and *value*. The team was ecstatic. ("The old man came here in person!") The department manager was publicly recognized in front of his whole team. And the exec bathed in the spotlight of success as well (after all, it was his hire who gave leadership to the difficult turnaround).

✓ ACTION STEP

How would you rate your relationship with your boss? How would you describe it—bad, tolerable, okay, average or excellent? Jot down a rating from one to ten for each of the thirteen suggestions for building a strong "boss" relationship. If you have a low rating for any of the points, list at least three things you can do to improve in that area. Use your ideas to set strategic goals to help you improve.

Rate from 1 to 10 ...

☐	Flex	☐	Take initiative
☐	Volunteer	☐	Produce
☐	Function autonomously	☐	Bring value
☐	Offer help	☐	Provide support
☐	Give cover	☐	Solve your boss's problems
☐	Take items off your boss's plate	☐	Get the boss enrolled in your projects
☐	Don't burn bridges		

Improvement:

CHAPTER 19:

Succeeding at your career

Effective leaders apply as much wisdom and effort to the stewardship of their careers as they do to their jobs. You must do the same. Take the "long look" and focus on your lifelong career goals. Above all, pay attention to yourself. Develop yourself into a valuable and marketable commodity. The good news for you as a worker is the emergence of a shrinking workforce—good people will become harder and harder for organizations to find, recruit, hire and retain. If you become one of those "good people," you'll find many wonderful opportunities for you to succeed and prosper in the coming economy. Decide right now that you are going to take advantage of that wonderful opportunity, and invest in your personal marketability. Follow the suggestions in this chapter to do just that.

1. **Perform like a star and act like one.** Don't focus on performance alone—pay close attention to your personal and professional image. Position yourself as a high-level professional. Be one of the best-dressed people at your level of the organization. (One industry expert coaches managers to "dress for the job you want, not the job you have.") Be neat and well-groomed, and be prepared to invest appropriately to do so. In other words, be willing to pay for good business attire, haircuts and the like. Get professional help to do so, if you need it.

   Make sure your nonverbal behaviors reflect a positive and enthusiastic attitude and mindset—walk and talk with confidence and self-assurance. Your physical state will also send a subliminal message to everyone who interacts with you, so send a positive message by maintaining your fitness and health. Demonstrate an attitude of success and professionalism by replacing all whining and complaining with a "can-do" spirit. It will help you to have an external frame of reference for all of this, so engage a trusted colleague to give you honest and direct feedback on your professional image. Ask a mentor for help with this, as well. Don't be sloppy about your work, and don't be sloppy about yourself.

2. **Look for opportunities to shine.** Here's one of the best pieces of advice I ever received in my career: *Opportunities are not created equal.* Some opportunities are better than others. Look for organizations, positions and jobs that give you a place to do your best work and really showcase your success. Sometimes it's a larger organization that will do that for you—a place that will look great on your résumé and open doors for even greater opportunity. Sometimes it's a smaller organization that will allow you quicker access to greater challenge and responsibility at a higher level. In any case, examine each situation carefully in the light of your goals for professional development and advancement. Remember: Visibility is essential to advancement and promotion. You want to find positions where higher-ups will be able to see and appreciate your success.

3. **Keep learning and growing.** In particular, keep learning about your work, your industry, the marketplace, your customers and your competition. But also focus on core competencies and strengths that are "transferable" to any organization or industry—leadership, management, organization, budget and finance, creativity, flexibility, etc. Use all the resources at your disposal to do this—books, audio series, professional associations, colleagues and mentors.

4. **Develop your people skills.** Your technical skills will take you only so far in your profession. To have the greatest impact, you must be able to function as an effective leader. To lead other people, you must have the requisite relational skills. Start by exploring and developing your own emotional intelligence. According to one expert, as much as 60% of your effectiveness on the job depends on your level of emotional intelligence! Expand that with an understanding of personality styles—the unique ways that different people express their passions, priorities, points of view and perceptions in the workplace. An understanding of generational, gender and cultural differences also will add to your leadership effectiveness. Groundbreaking research into failed executives surfaced a problem that was common to the great majority— their failure to form an effective personal "connection" with their team members. Don't make the same mistake. Build a sure foundation for certain success by acquiring the skills for healthy personal relationships.

5. **Sharpen your communication skills.** Everything you do as a leader depends on your ability to communicate effectively, personally, emotionally and persuasively on the job. So focus on developing better communication skills. In particular, develop the ability to speak well in front of a group, because the ability to deliver effective presentations is one of the single most promotable skills in organizations today. Studies of successful leaders have shown it's well worth your investment of time, energy and money to acquire this key executive skill.

6. **Build your network.** Start with your personal network. Cultivate supportive relationships with people you trust who will be there for you as sources of encouragement, wise counsel and healthy friendship. Studies show that less than one percent of leaders today have these kinds of relationships in their lives. Don't rely on your spouse to be your sole source of encouragement—build friendships with people in your industry or profession who understand your unique professional demands, stresses and problems. Use these special colleagues as sounding boards for your own decision-making, problem-solving and personal growth.

   Now build your professional network—the larger and wider, the better. Your professional network will be an important source of information and professional development. Your network will keep you in close touch with your profession or industry, resource your professional growth, help you find and recruit a mentor, provide a source for finding good people to hire and help you find job opportunities as well. Join an association connected with your industry, your profession or your role in the organization. If you find it difficult to meet and interact with people, get over it and force yourself to do it. Develop the skill to "meet and greet," and with practice, you'll feel more comfortable. Stay in touch with your network, and use e-mail, the phone and association events to maintain those all-important relationships. Use your professional network to find and recruit a mentor for your professional growth and development. Take advantage of the wisdom and experience of a successful person in your industry you admire and trust. Seek them out and ask if you can meet with them on a regular basis (monthly works well for most busy people) to use them as a sounding board and coach.

7. **Be a team player.** By all means, seek to shine as a star performer. But never do that at the expense of the team. Your greatest value to any organization will ultimately rest on the value you bring to it. Increasingly, that value comes from how you help the whole team succeed. If you develop the image and reputation of a maverick outsider, that is where you'll end up—on the outside. Ultimately, most executives aren't nearly as interested in having thoroughbreds in their stables as they are having strong horses on their *team*. One of the highest compliments I ever received as a leader came from the exec who told a board member, "I have never detected a personal agenda in him. Every time we talk, it's always about how the team and the organization can succeed."

8. **Stay positive.** When most people face the immovable object or irresolvable situation, they take one of two paths: Resentment or resignation. Make sure you choose the third path: Enthusiastic optimism! Every organization—and I mean every organization—has its share of persistent problems, bureaucratic obstacles, maddening dysfunctions and frustrating resistance. You'll never be effective as a leader if you descend into negativity—whining, complaining, blaming or criticizing. Your team needs a leader who will lead them to higher performance *in spite of* the obstacles they face. They need a leader who will say to them, "We must accept the difficult reality that we're dealing with and not expect it to change any day soon. So let's work together to find ways to do our work *in spite of* the obstacles before us!" That doesn't mean that you abandon truth and embrace denial—that is a prescription for leadership failure. It means that you become what Napoleon Bonaparte called "a dealer in hope." You become a leader who takes the team forward even in the midst of difficulty.

You must also apply the same mindset toward your own work and your own boss. Adopt a "can-do" spirit and tackle tough assignments with dogged determination, positive optimism and hard work. Most bosses aren't interested in hearing you complain. I once reported to a successful executive who detested any hint of whining or complaining from his team. He explained his point of view to a subordinate who complained of the difficulty of his assignment. He told this team member, "Of course your work is difficult—I didn't hire you to do the easy job. I could have hired any of a hundred other people to do that. I hired you to do the difficult job. So get busy and start doing it!"

9. **Stay objective.** Don't take anything in the workplace personally—maintain a healthy emotional distance from your work. Accept criticism positively and constructively. Don't let yourself get emotionally hooked into an angry reaction or response. Accept the reality of failure and take your mistakes in stride. Learn from your missteps—use them as opportunities to gain valuable wisdom and experience. Don't let your occasional stumbles defeat you personally or emotionally. Always put them in perspective—every leader fails at some point and in some ways. It happens. It will happen to you. Healthy leaders are able to continue forward in spite of their failures and not allow themselves to be judged *solely* on the basis of their mistakes.

10. **Draw attention to your success by praising everyone else's.** Nobody likes leaders who toot their own horn. No matter how well they do it, they always appear arrogant, shallow and self-centered. Take the high road instead. Make it your point to praise the accomplishments of everyone *around you*—colleagues, superiors and subordinates. When you give credit to others, it always reflects positively on *you*, probably because it's exactly what mature, self-confident people do. It also establishes you as a team player—someone who is more interested in the success of *all* of us. And when you praise the accomplishments of *your own team* to others, not only do your team members respond positively, *so do others*. You benefit in the process because your team's success is *your* success. Their success reflects well on their leader. It's simple—your team cannot succeed without good leadership. And so when they succeed, it proves they have a great leader!

11. **Groom and promote your people.** Some people believe that they should promote the view that they are indispensable or irreplaceable in their particular role of leadership in the organization. Nothing could be more damaging to your professional success. The truth is quite the opposite: If you want to be promoted, make it easy for higher-ups to find an adequate replacement—someone from your own team—someone you have personally prepared and trained for that role. Groom your team members for promotion and advancement. Train them. Give them assignments that will help develop their strengths and expand their skills. Help them find opportunities for advancement in the organization. If you gain the reputation of "star maker," it will add to your value and make you even more promotable. It also will make you the

boss that everyone wants to work for—you'll attract the brightest and best workers to your team, and you'll have your pick of the best candidates when it's time to hire. And hiring high performers will make it even easier for you to succeed as a leader.

UP CLOSE AND PERSONAL

Margaret was forcibly retired from her work in the health services industry because of a heart condition. When her husband died suddenly, she was forced to find new sources of income and a new direction for her professional life. She chose an opportunity to teach her practical professional skills at the community college level. She quickly discovered her talent for practical training and the lucrative potential for doing it without harming her health. She set ambitious career goals to acquire a full-time credential and the valuable advantages it would bring—health insurance and retirement benefits.

Over time, she completed her undergraduate degree, received a teaching credential, acquired a full-time class load, earned a post-graduate degree, and eventually became a department head. After "official retirement" from her community college career, she found continued opportunities to teach at local hospitals and health agencies where she could pursue her passion and supplement her modest retirement income. She also volunteered at local public schools as a tutor and mentor to students who found great value in her teaching skills. She discovered that her ambitious goals for a new career led to great benefits in her work and fulfilling experiences in an active (and impacting) retirement.

✓ACTION STEP

Write down your long-term career goals. Where do you want to go in your career? What do you want to accomplish? Even if you are close to retirement, think about those years still ahead of you. Write down your career goals. Put them down on paper. Share them with trusted friends and colleagues. Keep them in front of you—always present in your mind and in your conscious planning and working.

My long-term career goals:

1.

2.

3.

4.

5.

6.

7.

Review the suggestions listed in this chapter. Give yourself a rating for each one. Reflect on your lowest-rated areas, and list three things you can do to improve in each one. Craft your immediate goals around those ideas for improvement.

Especially if you are close to retirement, think about what you want to do after you complete your career—aside from endless rounds of golf or poolside lounging. How do you want to express your gifts and passions as a retired professional? What legacy do you want to leave? What contributions do you want to make? What value do you want to bring to the next generation or the world they will inherit? Now think about the things you can do right now in your work that will contribute to your after-retirement goals. You may be surprised at how relevant this thinking is to your current success!

A CLOSING WORD ...

Now it's your turn. You have the tools and information you need to improve your leadership and achieve greater success. The next step is up to you. Don't hesitate. Set aside time each week to apply the ideas and suggestions presented in each chapter. Start by working your way through the action steps. Share your intentions with your team and your circle of support. Set appropriate goals and start working your way toward them.

You can do it. You can become a better leader. Your team will benefit from your growth as a leader. So will your organization. Take the initiative. Start today.